"Dedicated to My Respected Grandfather"

'DADA'..........

About the Author

Prof. Dr. Amol B. Kasture received his M.C.A from University of Pune, India in 2008. He is having 6 years of experience in academic sector. He is member of following International Association.

1. Associate Senior Member of **UACEE** – Universal Association of Computer & Electronics Engineers.
2. Associate Life Member of **INAAR**- International Association of Academicians and Researchers.
3. Senior Member of **IEDRC**- International Economics Development Research Center.
4. Member of **AIRCC** – Software Engineering & Software Community.
5. Member of **IACSIT** – International Association of Computer Science & Information Technology.
6. Member of **SEEK** – SEEK Digital Library association with UACEE.
7. Member of **SSRN** – Social Science Research Network (Plus SSRN eLibrary).
8. Member of **IAENG**– International Association of Engineers.
9. Member of **SDIWC**– The Society of Digital Information and Wireless Communications.
10. Member of **ISOC**- Internet Society of Global Organization.
11. Member of **CSTA**- Computer Science Teachers Association.

He has completed his **Ph.D** in Computer Management in 2012 under the subject Software Engineering. Presently he is working as Assistant. Professor for MCA in P.E. Society's – Institute of Management & Career Development (MCA), Nigdi, Pune, Maharashtra, India. He has presented and published research paper in various States, National, International conferences and Journals. His research interests are Software Engineering, SDLC methodologies in SDLC, Wi-Fi Communication, and Data mining. He has published books on **"Expert in VB 6.0"** ,**"Training Guide of UML"** and **"Web Technology With HTML 5.0"**.

He has worked on AICTE Online Report process as well as CAP (Central Assessment Program), University of Pune of MBA, MCA & MCM. He has worked as Approved Committee Member of University of Pune for securing approval of UOP to upcoming MBA institute. He is also working as Paper Setter & Examiner for MCA, MBA, PGDBM courses in University of Pune.

Prof. Dr. AMOL B. KASTURE

(D.C.O., B.C.S., M.C.A., Cyber Law CS, Ph.D - Computer Mgt.)

Assistant Professor - MCA Department

P.E. Society's I.M.C.D. (MCA), Nigdi, Pune.

Dear Readers,

It gives me an immense pleasure to write comments on the book entitle **System Analysis & Design with Case Studies** written by **Dr. Amol B. Kasture.** This book contains total 14 chapters on System analysis and design, In this book language used by author is simple, lucid and covers the concept with example. The topics within the chapters have been arranged in a proper sequence to ensure smooth flow of the subject.

This book will be useful to the students to learn the concept and hands-on Software Engineering with Analysis and Design. It will be also useful to present System or Software as process and flow using various system design notation. Solved case studies and Examples will be helpful for self learning without taking experts guidance.

Best compliments for introducing valuable book on System Analysis & Design which is core part of Software Engineering.

Dr. Ramchandra G. Pawar
Ph.D.,M.C.A.(Engg.),M.P.M.,M.A. (Eco.), LL.B.(Spl.),B.Sc.(Phy.),DCL
Director
Sinhgad Institute of Business Administration and Computer Application (SIBACA)-MCA,
Lonavala, Dist – Pune 410401

Preface

My goal in writing this book is to provide a comprehensive guide to System Analysis and Design. What I will present for you is not just an overview of the Software Engineering, but a detailed look at the techniques required to analyze and design them for in real-world applications. I will look at the system analysis and design process for creating and building System or Application to make it all go.

Just as there is beauty in well-designed System. In fact, it is not possible to develop a System without understanding the System Analysis and Design concepts. You become involved with the development to a degree beyond that which is possible with software engineering. Best of all, it's a lot of fun.

As well as developing system, I have also taught courses in Software Engineering at Management Institute. There are many books out there on this topic, each book has its merits, and neglect the important issues of timing and design verification. For some time, I wanted to write a book that provided definitive coverage of developing application for real-world use. The opportunity to write for System Analysis and Design with Case Studies Edition first provided the happy circumstance, and thus this book was born.

Although I have taken maximum precautions, some errors might have creeped in. Constructive suggestions are welcome from readers.

"My special thanks to my parents, my wife, my son Ankit, my friends, my students & my respected Guru"

Prof. Dr. AMOL B. KASTURE

INDEX

Topic 1. Introduction about System Analysis & Design

- **Introduction:**

"System" if u heard this word what idea comes in mind; A System which is made up of subsystem, System is such a thing where you need to give something and you will get something and so on. Lots of idea and terms comes in mind About System. In standard way the system will state as "System is a collection of components that work together to achieve some objective forms a system".

Basically there are three major components in every system, namely input, processing and output.

Software Engineering is the systematic approach to the development, operation and maintenance of software. Software Engineering is concerned with development and maintenance of software products. The primary goal of software engineering is to provide the quality of software with low cost. Software Engineering involves project planning, project management, systematic analysis, design, validations and maintenance activities.

Assuming that a new system is to be developed, the next phase is system analysis. Analysis involved a detailed study of the current system, leading to specifications of a new system. Analysis is a detailed study of various operations performed by a system and their relationships within and outside the system. During analysis, data are collected on the available files, decision points and transactions handled by the present system. Interviews, on-site observation and questionnaire are the tools used for system analysis. Using the following steps it becomes easy to draw the exact boundary of the new system under consideration:

- Keeping in view the problems and new requirements
- Workout the pros and cons including new areas of the system

Based on the user requirements and the detailed analysis of a new system, the new system must be designed. This is the phase of **system designing**. It is a most crucial phase in the development of a system. Normally, the design proceeds in two stages:

- preliminary or general design
- Structure or detailed design

Preliminary or general design: In the preliminary or general design, the features of the new system are specified.

- **NEED FOR SYSTEMS ANALYSIS AND DESIGN**

Systems analysis and design, as performed by systems analysts, seeks to understand what humans need to analyze data input or data flow systematically, process or transform data, store data, and output information in the context of a particular business. Furthermore, systems analysis and design is used to analyze, design, and implement improvements in the support of users and the functioning of Businesses that can be accomplished through the use of computerized information systems. Installing a system without proper planning leads to great user dissatisfaction and frequently causes the system to fall into disuse. Systems analysis and design lends structure to the analysis and design of information systems, a costly endeavor that might otherwise have been done in a random way. It can be thought of as a series of processes systematically undertaken to improve a business through the use of computerized information systems. Systems analysis and design involves working with current and eventual users of information systems to support them in working with technologies in an organizational setting. User involvement throughout the systems project is critical to the successful development of computerized information systems. Systems analysts, whose roles in the organization are discussed next, are the other essential component in developing useful information systems.

Users are moving to the forefront as software development teams become more international in their composition. This means that there is more emphasis on working with software users; on performing analysis of their business, problems, and objectives; and on communicating the analysis and design of the planned system to all involved.

New technologies also are driving the need for systems analysis. Ajax is not a new programming language, but a technique that uses existing languages to make Web pages function more like a traditional desktop application program. Building and redesigning Web pages that utilize Ajax technologies will be a task facing analysts. New programming languages, such as Ruby on Rails, which is a combination programming language and code generator for creating Web applications, will require more analysis.

- **System Analysis & Design:**

System Analysis:

Systems analysis is the study of sets of interacting entities, including computer systems analysis. All procedures, requirements must be analyzed and documented in the form of detailed data flow diagrams (DFDs), data dictionary, logical data structures and miniature specifications. System Analysis also includes sub-dividing of complex process involving the entire system, identification of data store and manual processes.

The main points to be discussed in system analysis are:

- Specification of what the new system is to accomplish based on the user requirements.
- Functional hierarchy showing the functions to be performed by the new system and their relationship with each other.
- Function network which are similar to function hierarchy but they highlight those functions which are common to more than one procedure.
- List of attributes of the entities - these are the data items which need to be held about each entity (record)

System Design:

The purpose of System Design is to create a technical solution that satisfies the functional requirements for the system. At this point in the project lifecycle there should be a Functional Specification, written primarily in business terminology, containing a complete description of the operational needs of the various organizational entities that will use the new system. The challenge is to translate all of this information into Technical Specifications that accurately describe the design of the system, and that can be used as input to System Construction.
The Functional Specification produced during System Requirements Analysis is transformed into a physical architecture. System components are distributed across the physical architecture, usable interfaces are designed and prototyped, and Technical Specifications are created for the Application Developers, enabling them to build and test the system.

Structure or Detailed design: In the detailed design stage, computer oriented work begins in earnest. At this stage, the design of the system becomes more structured. Structure design is a blue print of a computer system solution to a given problem having the same components and inter-relationship among the same components as the original problem.

Input, output and processing specifications are drawn up in detail. In the design stage, the programming language and the platform in which the new system will run are also decided.

There are several tools and techniques used for designing. These tools and techniques are:

1. Flow Chart

2. Data Flow Diagram (DFD)

3. Entity Relationship Diagram (ERD)

3. Decision Table

4. Decision Tree

Software Requirement specification is part of System preparation; in short we will define SRS as is a comprehensive description of the intended purpose and environment for software under development. The SRS fully describes what the software will do and how it will be expected to perform.

We will see System Design & SRS concept with case studies in next chapters which will cover the FDD, ERD, DFD, DATA DICTIONARY, SRS (How to make SRS).

-----------------------**End**-------------------------

Note:

Topic 2. Entity Relationship Diagram

- **Introduction:**

    ERD is one of the Data models are tools used in analysis to describe the data requirements and assumptions in the system from a top-down perspective. They also set the stage for the design of databases later on in the SDLC.

Definition:-

    "It is also called an entity-relationship model, a graphical representation of entities and their relationships to each other, typically used in computing in regard to the organization of data within databases or information systems."

OR

    "An entity-relationship diagram is a data modeling technique that creates a graphical representation of the entities, and the relationships between entities, within an information system."

The three main components of an ERD are:

- The entity :

    It is a person, object, place or event for which data is collected. For example, if you consider the information system for a business, entities would include not only customers, but the customer's address, and orders as well. The entity is represented by a rectangle and labeled with a singular noun.

- The relationship:

This is the interaction between the entities. In the example above, the customer places an order, so the word "places" defines the relationship between that instance of a customer and the order or orders that they place. A relationship may be represented by a diamond shape, or more simply, by the line connecting the entities. In either case, verbs are used to label the relationships.

- The cardinality :

Defines the relationship between the entities in terms of numbers. An entity may be optional: for example, a sales rep could have no customers or could have one or many customers; or mandatory: for example, there must be at least one product listed in an order. There are several different types of cardinality notation; crow's foot notation, used here, is a common one. In crow's foot notation, a single bar indicates one, a double bar indicates one and only one (for example, a single instance of a product can only be stored in one warehouse), a circle indicates zero, and a crow's foot indicates many. The three main cardinal relationships are:

one-to-one, expressed as 1:1;

one-to-many, expressed as 1:M;

and many-to-many, expressed as M:N.

The steps involved in creating an ERD are:

- Identify the entities.
- Determine all significant interactions.
- Analyze the nature of the interactions.
- Draw the ERD.

What are Entity Relationship Diagrams?

Entity Relationship Diagrams (ERDs) illustrate the logical structure of databases.

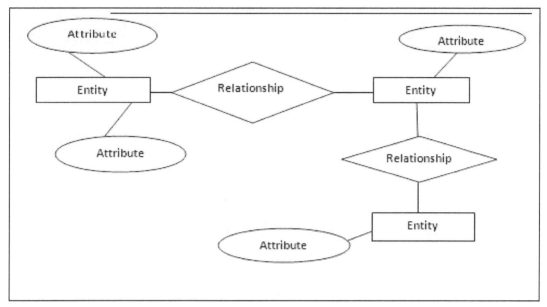

An ER Diagram

Entity Relationship Diagram Notations

Peter Chen developed ERDs in 1976. Since then Charles Bachman and James Martin have added some slight refinements to the basic ERD principles.

1. Entity

An entity is an object or concept about which you want to store information.

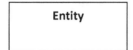

2. Weak Entity

A weak entity is an entity that must defined by a foreign key relationship with another entity as it cannot be uniquely identified by its own attributes alone.

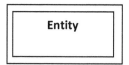

3. Key attribute

A key attribute is the unique, distinguishing characteristic of the entity. For example, an employee's social security number might be the employee's key attribute.

4. Multivalued attribute

A multivalued attribute can have more than one value. For example, an employee entity can have multiple skill values.

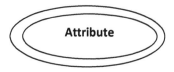

5. Derived attribute

A derived attribute is based on another attribute. For example, an employee's monthly salary is based on the employee's annual salary.

6. Relationships

Relationships illustrate how two entities share information in the database structure.

Learn how to draw relationships:
First, connect the two entities, then drop the relationship notation on the line.

7. Cardinality

Cardinality specifies how many instances of an entity relate to one instance of another entity.

Ordinarily is also closely linked to cardinality. While cardinality specifies the occurrences of a relationship, cardinality describes the relationship as either mandatory or optional. In other words, cardinality specifies the maximum number of relationships and cardinality specifies the absolute minimum number of relationships.

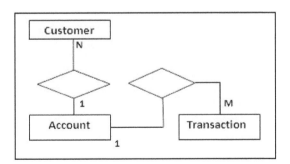

8. Recursive relationship

In some cases, entities can be self-linked. For example, employees can supervise other employees.

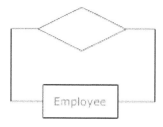

Cardinality Notations

Cardinality specifies how many instances of an entity relate to one instance of another entity. Ordinarily is also closely linked to cardinality. While cardinality specifies the occurrences of a relationship, cordiality describes the relationship as either mandatory or optional. In other words, cardinality specifies the maximum number of relationships and cordiality specifies the absolute minimum number of relationships. When the minimum number is zero, the relationship is usually called optional and when the minimum number is one or more, the relationship is usually called mandatory.

Information Engineering

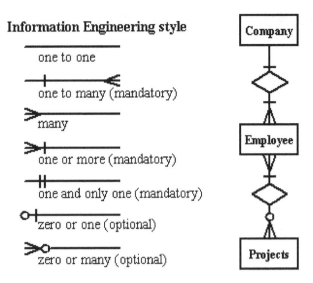

Information Engineering style

one to one

one to many (mandatory)

many

one or more (mandatory)

one and only one (mandatory)

zero or one (optional)

zero or many (optional)

Company

Employee

Projects

- **Creating an Entity/Relationship Diagram**

The ERD is constructed in an iterative manner. The following approach is taken:

1. During requirements elicitation, customers are asked to list the "things" that the application or business process addresses. These "things" evolve into a list of input and output data objects as well as external entities that produce or consumer information.

2. Taking the objects one at a time, the analyst and customer define whether or not a connection (unnamed at this stage) exists between the data object and other objects.

3. Wherever a connection exists, the analyst and the customer create one or more object/relationship pairs.

4. For each object/relationship pair, cardinality and modality are explored.

5. Steps 2 through 4 are continued iteratively until all object/relationships have been defined. It is common to discover omissions as this process continues. New objects and relationships will invariably be added as the number of iterations grows.

6. The attributes of each entity are defined.

7. An entity relationship diagram is formalized and reviewed.

8. Steps 1 through 7 are repeated until data modeling is complete.

- **Difference Between ERD and DFD**

ERD and DFD are models of data presentation in the fact that help identify the flow of data as well as inputs and outputs. They are important as they allow effective communication between members of different departments in an organization. There are similarities in both types of models have data although

The DFD's is the systematic representation of how the data flow in an organization, how and from where it enters the system, how it moves from one process to another and how it is kept in the organization. On the other hand, a semantic data model of a system in a top to bottom as the Diagram or ERD Entity Report. ERD shows how a system will look like without saying how to run it. Since it is based entity, ERD shows the relationship between entities in a system or process. Furthermore, the flow charts being DRD data focuses on the flow of data in a system and how this data is used in different stages of a process.

Both DFD & ERD are important to an organization. As entities, they are the people, places, events or objects are represented in an ERD, DFD discussions of how the data flow between entities. It is knowledge of the entities for which data is stored in the organization by ERD as DFD provides information on the flow of data between entities and how and where it is kept. Different instruments are capitalized and preparing DFD & ERD. While it is common to use circles, ovals, rectangles and arrows to DFD, ERD uses only rectangles boxes. Diamonds are used to represent relationships between entities in ERD and find the description of the report as a list in DFD is a simple word. Despite their popularity and widespread use, both DFD & ERD are incomplete in the sense that we do not receive the complete picture looking any of the two diagrams to represent data.

Sample E-R Diagram

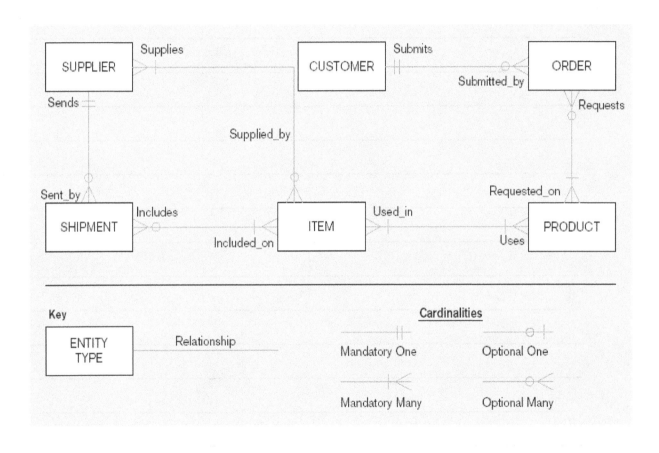

----------------------End------------------------

Topic 3. Functional Decomposition Diagram

- **Introduction:**

A method of business analysis that dissects a complex business process to show its individual elements. Functional decomposition is used to facilitate the understanding and management of large and or complex processes and can be used to help solve problem. Functional decomposition is used in computer engineering to help with software design.

Definition:-

- **Decomposition:**

"The breakdown of matter by bacteria and fungi, changing the chemical makeup and physical appearance of materials."

OR

"The process of breaking the description of a system down into small components; also called functional decomposition".

- **Decomposition diagram:**

A decomposition diagram shows a

- high-level function,
- process, organization,
- data subject area,
- or another type of object

The diagram shows it broken down into lower level, more detailed components.

- **A decomposition diagram does not show:**

1. The order of carrying out tasks
2. Dependency between blocks
3. Movements between blocks.

- **Drawing a Decomposition Diagram**

Step 1: Identifying high level process.

Step 2: Then break them down into sub-process until they cannot be decomposed or broken down any further.

Step 3: Each process has an action word in it such as

- Add
- Delete
- Sort
- Search

Organizations perform a variety of different functions. Traditionally, managers thought of the functions of a business as departments, such as Marketing, Finance, and Accounting. However, they are beginning to view business functions as important processes that occur throughout the organization's value chain, which is the series of interdependent activities that bring a product or service to the customer. For example, value chain activities may include inbound logistics, operations, marketing and sales, and order fulfillment.

Before an analyst can plan what systems to build for the organization, it is helpful to first understand the business functions that the organization needs to perform. Then it is much easier to identify processes that occur within the business functions, and ultimately the systems that will support those processes. This is a top-down approach to systems development.

Overview of Functional Decomposition Diagram (FDD)

- A primary functional analysis technique is the Functional Decomposition Diagram (FDD).
- Purpose: to show the sequential relationship of all functions that must be accomplished by a system.
- Each function (represented by a block) is identified and described in terms of *inputs, outputs, and interfaces* from *top down* so that sub-functions are recognized as part of larger functional areas.
- Some functions may be performed in *parallel*, or *alternate paths* may be be taken.
- Functions are arranged in a *logical sequence* so that any specified operational use of the system can be traced in an end-to-end path.
- The FDD network shows the logical sequence of "*what*" must happen, and does not assume a particular answer to "how" a function will be performed.

Functional Decomposition is a technique of taking a business function and breaking it down into sub-functions. A Functional Decomposition Diagrams is a structure chart that shows the functions and sub-functions all in a single view. It normally does not show process flow, information flow, logic flow, or anything else – just the decomposition. As business processes are connected to enterprise value chains, often the high-level definitions are not suitable for computer implementation. Process decomposition is a technique to break-down high level process definitions into finer grain (sub) processes. The decomposition is repeated several times, for example, starting from business function, to process groups, to core business processes, to business activities, to a task, and finally to a step.

- **Functional Decomposition Diagram or Functional Charts Example:**

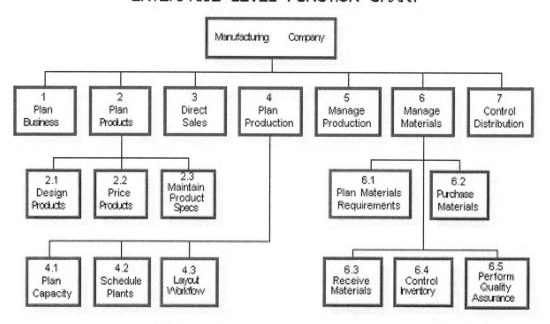

1. FDD for Manufacturing Company

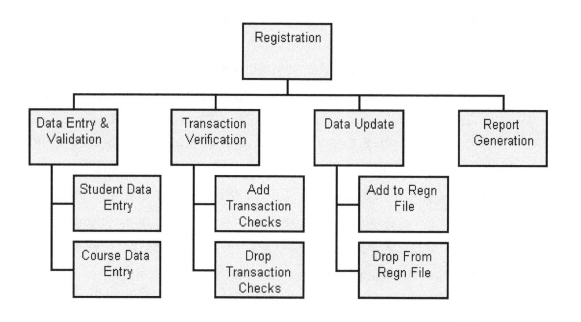

2. FDD for Student Registration System

- **A General view of drawing an FDD**

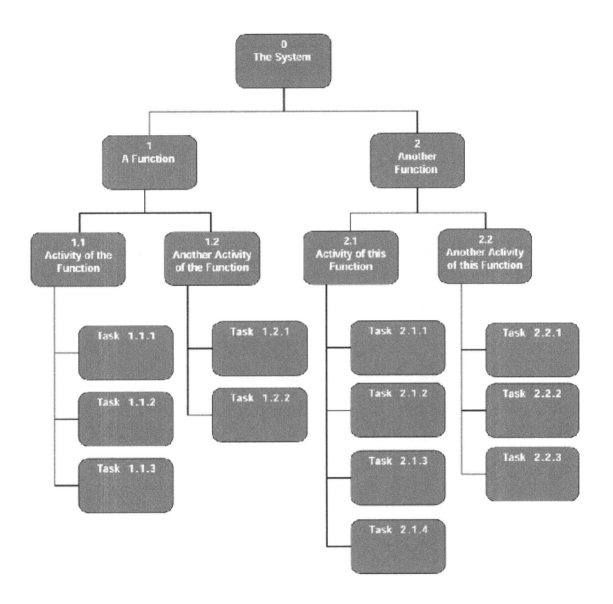

Decomposition is the act of breaking a system into its component subsystems, processes, and sub-processes. Each level of abstraction reveals more or less detail.

A decomposition diagram or hierarchy chart shows the top-down, functional decomposition of a system.

- **Use Functional Decomposition to:**

- Hierarchically decompose a system into its functional components,
- Hierarchically decompose a <u>business process</u> into sub-processes,
- Provide a definition of all the <u>business functions</u> and sub-functions identified as system requirements.

CONSIDERATIONS WHEN DRAWING FUNCTION DECOMPOSITION DIAGRAM

1. Levels on a Function Chart

A level of a Function Chart is composed of functions or business processes. Do not mix functions and business processes on the same level. Each lower level of the Function Chart provides details for the level immediately above. Lower levels are a decomposition of the upper level business function or business process, not separate from the upper level. Complete the subordinates for any one function before further exploding any of the subordinates. For example, if a subordinate of the function Accounting is Pay Bill, identify all subordinates of Accounting before further decomposing Pay Bill. Administrative services or utility functions are not typically top level functions.

2. Rule of Thumb for Number of Subordinates

As a rule of thumb, limit the number of subordinates of a function to seven. If there are more, group related subordinates and explode them in a lower level. For example, the function Finance may have subordinates Funds Management, Cash, Short-Term Financing, Long-Term Financing, Financial Control, Budget, Managerial Accounting, and General Accounting. To limit the number of subordinates under Finance, you may combine Managerial Accounting and General Accounting under Accounting and explode them at the next level.

3. Function Chart Numbering Scheme

Use a hierarchical numbering scheme. For example, if the function Accounting is numbered 1 on the chart, successive breakdowns of Accounting would be numbered 1.1, 1.2, 1.1.1, and so on.

4. Tip for Numbering Function Chart

When numbering the charts, remember that function numbers are just a label and have no meaning. However, the specifications document will likely be organized by function number. Therefore, it is a good idea to assign the low numbers to the functions that should appear first in the document. Otherwise, top level users may not understand that what they consider to be the organization's most important function is, for example, number ten and starts on page 183 of the document.

----------------------End----------------------

Note:

Topic 4. Data Flow Diagram

- **Introduction:**

A DFD is one of the three essential perspectives of Structured Systems Analysis and Design Method (SSADM). In this method, both the project sponsors and the end users need to collaborate closely throughout the whole stages of the evolution of the system. Having a DFD will make the collaboration easy because the end users will be able to visualize the operation of the system, the will see a better perspective what the system will accomplish and how the whole project will be implemented.

A project implementation can also be made more efficient especially in progress monitoring. The DFD of the old system can be laid side by side with the new system's DFD so that comparisons can be made and weak points can be identified so that the appropriate innovations can be developed.

Definition:-

"A DFD illustrates those functions that must be performed in a program as

well as the data that the function will need."

OR

"Data Flow Diagram (DFD) is an important technique for modeling a system's high-level detail by showing how input data is transformed to output results through a sequence of functional transformations."

- **Why DFDs are useful?**

When it comes to conveying how information data flows through system and how that data is transformed in the process, DFDs are the method of choice over technical descriptions for three principle reasons.

1. DFDs are easier to understand by technical and non-technical audiences
2. DFDs can provide a high level system overview, complete with boundaries and connections to other systems
3. DFDs can provide a detailed representation of system components.

- A data flow diagram represents the following:

1. External devices sending and receiving data
2. Processes that change that data
3. Data flows themselves
4. Data storage locations

- **Components of DFD**

There are four components of a data flow diagram which are the following:

1. **External Entities / Terminators** - These refer or points to the outside parts of the system being developed or modeled. Terminators, depending on whether data flows into or from the system, are often called sinks or sources. They represent the information as wherever it comes from or where it goes.

2. **Processes** – The Processes component modifies the inputs and corresponding outputs.

3. **Data Stores** – refers to any place or area or storage where data will be placed whether temporarily or permanently.

4. **Data Flows** – refers to the way data will be transferred from one terminator to another, or through processes and data stores.

- **How to draw a DFD? or Built a Data Flow Diagram**

There only four symbols used to write Data Flow Diagram as follows:

Components	Symbol Used	Notation
External Entities	Rectangular box	
Data Flow	Arrow headed lines	
Process	Bubble (Circle or round corner square)	**OR**
Data Store	Narrow opened rectangle	

A general Rules for drawing DFD:

1. every page in a DFD should not contain more than 10 components. So, if there are more than 10 components in one processes, one or more components should have to be combined and then make another DFD to detail the combination in another page.

2. Each component needs to be number. Same goes for each subcomponent so that it will be easy to follow visually. For example, a top level DFD must have components numbered 1,2,3,4,5 and next level subcomponent (for instance of number 2) numbered 2.1, 2.2, 2.3 and so on.

3. There are two approaches to developing a DFD. The first approach is the Top Down Approach where a DFD starts with a context level DVD and then the system is slowly decomposed until the graphical detail goes down to a primitive level.

- **During the analysis stage of a project it is important to find out how data flows through a system:**

    ✓ Where does the data originate ?
    ✓ What processing is performed on it and by whom ?
    ✓ Who uses the data ?
    ✓ What data is stored and where ?
    ✓ What output is produced and who receives it ?

- **Drawing an Data Flow Diagram (DFD)**

Context Diagram Guidelines

Step 1. Firstly, draw and name a single process box that represents the entire system.

Step 2. Next, identify and add the external entities that communicate directly with the process box. Do this by considering origin and destination of the resource flows and data flows.

Step 3. Finally, add the resource flows and data flows to the diagram.

In drawing the context diagram you should only be concerned with the most important information flows. Remember that no business process diagram is the definitive solution - there is no absolute right or wrong.

Document flow analysis is particularly useful where information flows are of special interest. The first step is to list the major documents and their sources and recipients. This is followed by the identification of other major information flows such as telephone and computer transactions. Once the document flow diagram has been drawn the system boundary should be added.

- **The procedure for producing a data flow diagram**

1. Identify the data connections between business functions.
2. confirm through personal contact sent data is received and vice-versa.
3. trace and record what happens to each of the data flows entering the system (data movement, data storage, data transformation/processing)
4. Draw an overview DFD
   - Shows the major subsystems and how they interact with one another
   - Exploding processes should add detail while retaining the essence of the

     details from the more general diagram
   - Consolidate all data stores into a composite data store

5. Draw middle-level DFDs
   - Explode the composite processes
6. Draw primitive-level DFDs
   - Detail the primitive processes
   - Must show all appropriate primitive data stores and data flows
7. Verify all data flows have a source and destination.
8. Verify data coming out of a data store goes in.
9. Review with "informed".
10. Explode and repeat above steps as needed.

   ✓ **Balancing DFDs**

   1. Balancing: child diagrams must maintain a balance in data content with their parent processes

      Can be achieved by either:

   2. exactly the same data flows of the parent process enter and leave the child diagram, or

3. the same net contents from the parent process serve as the initial inputs and final outputs for the child diagram or
4. the data in the parent diagram is split in the child diagram

Rules for Drawing DFDs

- A process must have at least one input and one output data flow
- A process begins to perform its tasks as soon as it receives the necessary input data flows
- A primitive process performs a single well-defined function
- Never label a process with an IF-THEN statement
- Never show time dependency directly on a DFD
- Be sure that data stores, data flows, data processes have descriptive titles. Processes should use imperative verbs to project action.
- All processes receive and generate at least one data flow.
- Begin/end data flows with a bubble.

Rules for Data Flows

- A data store must always be connected to a process
- Data flows must be named
- Data flows are named using nouns
  " Customer ID, Student information"
- Data that travel together should be one data flow
- Data should be sent only to the processes that need the data

Use the following additional guidelines when drawing DFDs

- Identify the key processing steps in a system. A processing step is an activity that transforms one piece of data into another form.
- Process bubbles should be arranged from top left to bottom right of page.
- Number each process (1.0, 2.0, etc). Also name the process with a verb that describes the information processing activity.
- Name each data flow with a noun that describes the information going into

and out of a process. What goes in should be different from what comes out.

- Data stores, sources and destinations are also named with nouns.
- Realize that the highest level DFD is the context diagram. It summarizes the entire system as one bubble and shows the inputs and outputs to a system.

- Each lower level DFD must balance with its higher level DFD. This means that no inputs and outputs are changed.

- Think of data flow not control flow. Data flows are pathways for data. Think about what data is needed to perform a process or update a data store. A data flow diagram is not a flowchart and should not have loops or transfer of control. Think about the data flows, data processes, and data storage that are needed to move a data structure through a system.
- Do not try to put everything you know on the data flow diagram. The diagram should serve as index and outline. The index/outline will be "fleshed out" in the data dictionary, data structure diagrams, and procedure specification techniques.

Data flow diagrams (DFDs) reveal relationships among and between the various components in a program or system. DFDs are an important technique for modeling a system's high-level detail by showing how input data is transformed to output results through a sequence of functional transformations. DFDs consist of four major components: entities, processes, data stores, and data flows. The symbols used to depict how these components interact in a system are simple and easy to understand; however, there are several DFD models to work from, each having its own symbology. DFD syntax does remain constant by using simple verb and noun constructs. Such a syntactical relationship of DFDs makes them ideal for object-oriented analysis and parsing functional specifications into precise DFDs for the systems analyst.

Context Level Data Flow Diagrams

A context diagram is a top level (also known as Level 0) data flow diagram. It only contains one process node (process 0) that generalizes the function of the entire system in relationship to external entities.

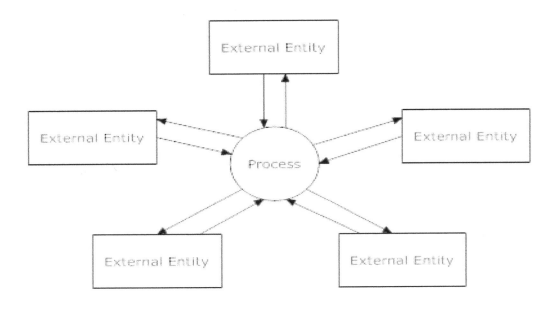

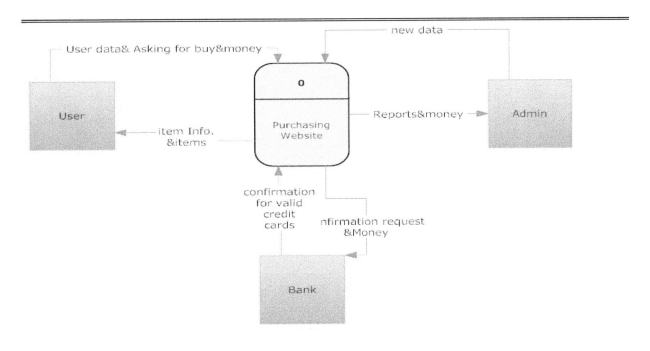

Context

• Examples of Data Flow Diagrams

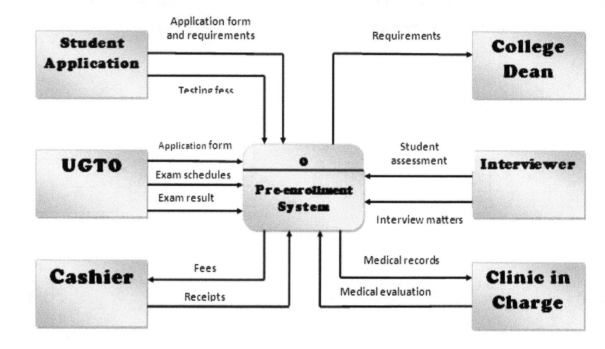

1. DFD for Pre Enrollment Systrem

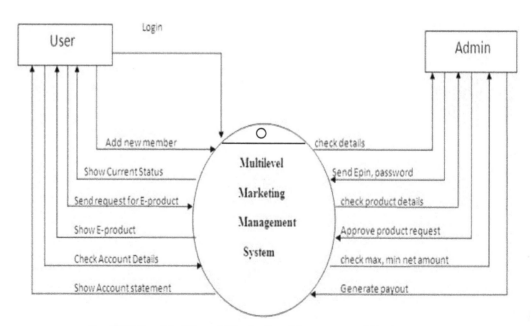

2. DFD For Multilevel Marketing Management System

-----------------------End-------------------------

Topic 5. Levels of DFD

- **Introduction to Logical and Physical Data Flow Diagrams**

Data flow diagrams (DFDs) are categorized as either logical or physical. A logical DFD focuses on the business and how the business operates. It describes the business events that take place and the data required and produced by each event. On the other hand, a physical DFD shows how the system will be implemented .logical model reflects the business, while the physical model depicts the system.

- **Types of Data Flow Diagram**

There are two types of data flow diagrams, namely physical data flow diagrams and logical data flow diagrams and it is important to distinguish clearly between the two:

1. Physical Data Flow Diagrams
An implementation-dependent view of the current system, showing what tasks are carried out and how they are performed. Physical characteristics can include:

Names of people

Form and document names or numbers

Names of departments

Master and transaction files

Equipment and devices used

Locations,Names of procedures

2. Logical Data Flow Diagrams

An implementation-*in*dependent view of the system, focusing on the flow of data between processes without regard for the specific devices, storage locations or people in the system. The physical characteristics listed above for physical data flow diagrams will not be specified.

- **Data Flow Diagram - Physical DFD to Logical DFD Conversion**

Physical DFDs are a means to an end, not an end in them. They are drawn to describe an implementation of the existing system for two reasons:

- To ensure a correct understanding of the current implementation (users are generally better able to discuss the physical system as they know it through people, workstations and days of the week.)

- The implementation itself may be a problem or limiting factor; changing the implementation, rather than the system concept may provide the desired results.

A logical view steps back from the actual implementation and provides a basis for examining the combination of processes, data flows, data stores, inputs and outputs without concern for the physical devices, people or control issues that characterise the implementation.

A logical data flow diagram is derived from the physical version by doing the following:

- Show actual *data* needed in a process, not the documents that contain them.

- Remove routing information; that is, show the flow between *procedures*, not between people, offices or locations.

- Remove references to physical devices.

- Remove references to control information

- Consolidate redundant data stores.

- Remove unnecessary processes, such as those that do not change the data or data flows.

- **Levels of DFD:**

  1. <u>**Context or Level 0 Diagram**</u>
  2. <u>**1st Level or Level 1 Diagram**</u>
  3. <u>**2nd Level or Level 2 Diagram**</u>

1. Context or Level 0 Diagram

The highest level view of a system. This only has one process which represents the overall function of the system and has no data stores as all the data is stored within the process.

Main steps when constructing a Level 0 Diagram:

Step 1: Identify where data is captured from

Step 2: Identify where data is distributed to

Step 3: Describe the overall process

Step 4: Map these out in a diagram using the correct symbols

Step 5: Link them with data flows that are labelled

2. 1st Level or Level 1 Diagram

This is the next level after context level view of a system.

Main steps when constructing a Level 1 Diagram :

Step 1: Identify and draw the processes that make up the Level 0 process

Step 2: Allocate descriptions to these.

Step 3: Lay out the sources/sinks and data flows from the Level 0 diagram

Step 4: Draw in any data stores used in the process.

Step 5: Link the new processes and data stores with named data links

3. **2nd or 3rd Level or Level 2 or 3 Diagram**

IF it is necessary to produce a level 2 or level 3 diagram, the same steps would be followed as used when constructing the Level 1 diagram.

- **Step wise Construction of Context (0TH) Level And 1st Level DFD**

Here is an example of how Data flow diagrams would be used to model the logic of data flows in a fast food burger bar.

✓ **Context or Level 0 Diagram =>**

Step 1: Identify where data is captured from

```
┌─────────────────────┐
│                     │
│      CUSTOMER       │
│                     │
└─────────────────────┘
```

Step 2: Identify where data is distributed to

```
┌──────────────────┐          ┌──────────────────┐
│  CUSTOMER        │          │  KITCHEN         │
│                  │          │                  │
└──────────────────┘          └──────────────────┘
```

```
┌──────────────────┐
│  RESTAURANT      │
│  MANAGER         │
│                  │
└──────────────────┘
```

Step 3: Describe the overall process

Step 4: Map these out in a diagram using the correct symbols

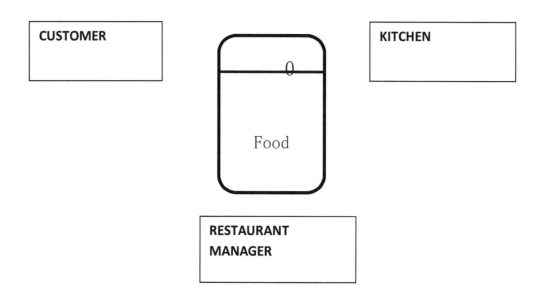

Step 5: Link them with data flows that are labelled

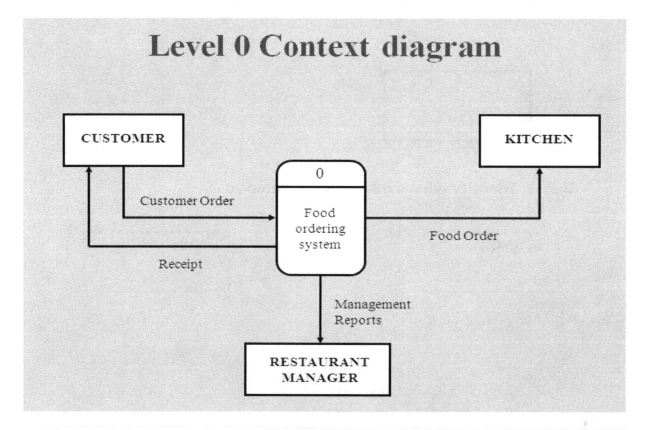

Step 1: Identify and draw the processes that make up the Level 0 process

Step 2: Allocate descriptions to these.

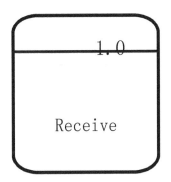

Step 3: Maintaining data stores

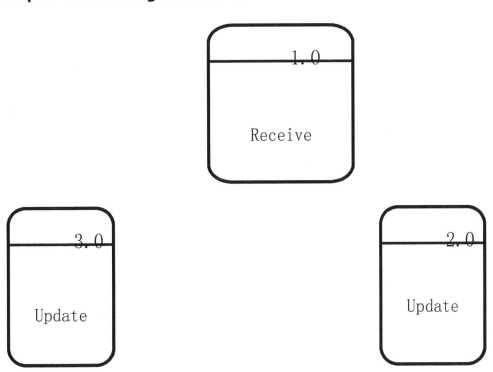

Step 3: Lay out the sources/sinks and data flows from the Level 0 diagram

Step 4: Draw in any data stores used in the process.

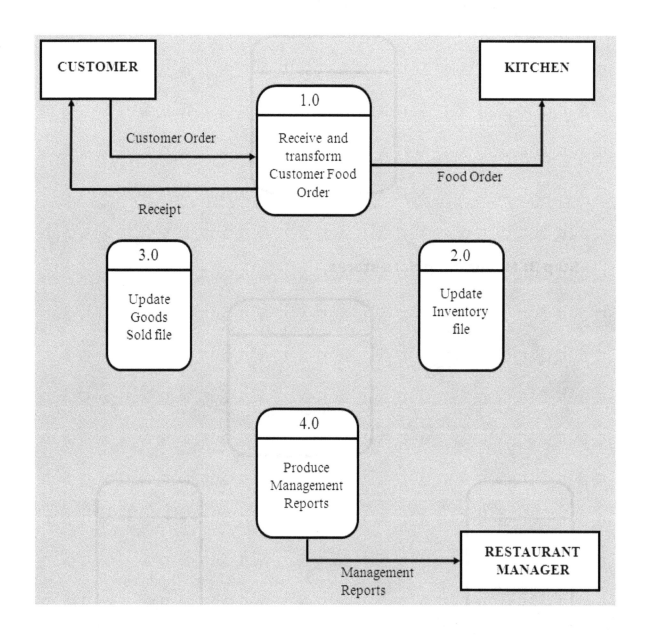

Step 5: Link the new processes and data stores with named data links

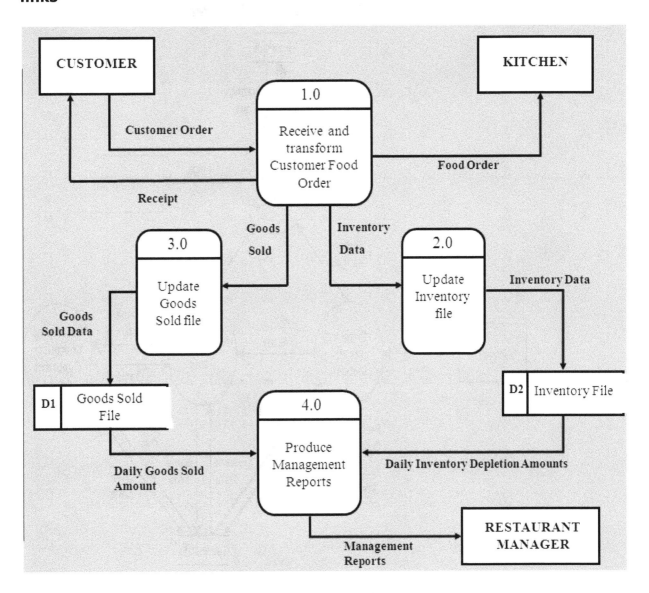

1ST Level DFD

✓ **2nd Level or Level 2 Diagram =>**

Example of 2nd Level DFD

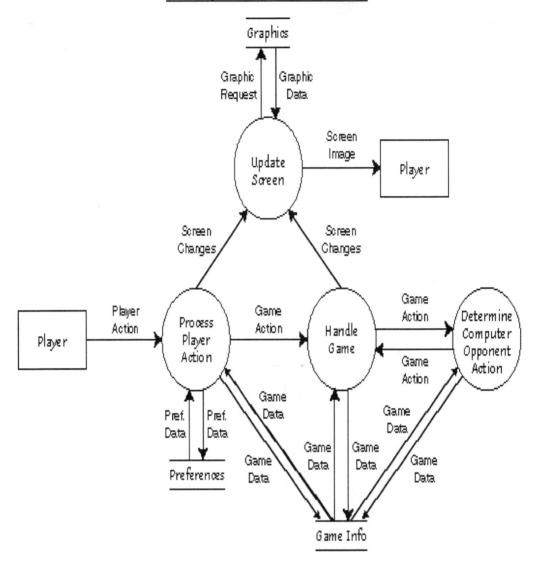

- **Benefits of DFD's**
1. Provide a pictorial , non- technical presentations
2. Are easy to understand
3. Quick to procedure & easy to amend
4. Use limited number of symbols with specific meanings
5. Use a simple, top town expansion.

----------------------End-------------------------

Note:

Topic 6. Decision Tree

- **Introduction of Decision Tree**

A decision tree can be used as a model for sequential decision problems under uncertainty. A decision tree describes graphically the decisions to be made, the events that may occur, and the outcomes associated with combinations of decisions and events. Probabilities are assigned to the events, and values are determined for each outcome. A major goal of the analysis is to determine the best decisions. Decision tree models include such concepts as nodes, branches, terminal values, strategy, payoff distribution, certain equivalent, and the rollback method.

Decision trees can be drawn by hand or created with a graphics program or specialized software. Informally, decision trees are useful for focusing discussion when a group must make a decision. Programmatically, they can be used to assign monetary/time or other values to possible outcomes so that decisions can be automated.

Definition:-

- **Decision Tree:**

"A decision tree is a graph that uses a branching method to illustrate every possible outcome of a decision.."

OR

"A schematic tree-shaped diagram used to determine a course of action or show a statistical probability. Each branch of the decision tree represents a possible decision or occurrence. The tree structure shows how one choice leads to the next, and the use of branches indicates that each option is mutually exclusive.".

> Here's a simple example: An email management decision tree might begin with a box labeled "Receive new message." From that, one branch leading off might lead to "Requires immediate response." From there, a "Yes" box leads to a single decision: "Respond." A "No" box leads to "Will take less than three minutes to answer" or "Will take more than three minutes to answer." From the first box, a box leads to "Respond" and from the second box, a branch leads to "Mark as task and assign priority." The branches might converge after that to "Email responded to? File or delete message."

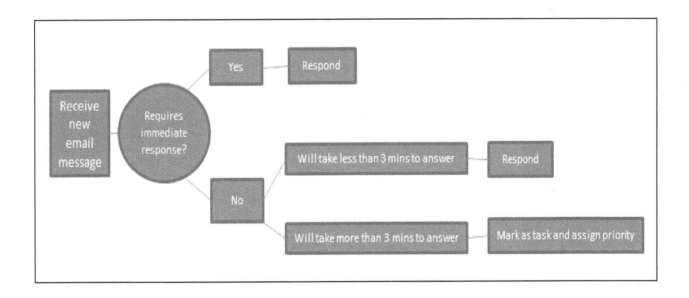

- **Why Decision Tree are useful?**

1. Decision Trees are excellent tools for helping you to choose between several courses of action. They provide a highly effective structure within which you can lay out options and investigate the possible outcomes of choosing those options. They also help you to form a balanced picture of the risks and rewards associated with each possible course of action.

2. Decision trees are a form of multiple variable (or multiple effect) analyses. All forms of multiple variable analyses allow us to predict, explain, describe, or classify an outcome (or target).

3. Decision trees attempt to find a strong relationship between input values and target values in a group of observations that form a data set.

4. Decision Trees are excellent tools for helping you to choose between several courses of action.

- **How to Make a Decision Tree?**

Following Notation are used to draw the Decision Tree:

Symbol Used	Description	Notation
Box	A box represents a **decision node**.	
Circle	A circle represents a **chance node**.	
Horizontal rectangle	A horizontal rectangle represents a **terminal node**.	

Note:-

- A box represents a **decision node**. Lines from the box denote the decision alternatives (one line per decision alternative). The name of the decision alternative goes above the line.

- A circle represents a **chance node**. Lines from the circle denote the events that could occur at the chance node. The name of the chance-driven event goes above the line. The probability of the event goes below the line. Since all probabilities at a chance node must sum to 1.0, one event is labeled simply as #, to denote "1 - the sum of the probabilities of the other events."

- A horizontal rectangle represents a **terminal node**. A terminal node represents an outcome state, so there are no events that occur distal to a terminal node. The value of the outcome appears in the rectangle. \

- **Rules for Drawing Decision Tree:-**

  Step 1. Start with your decision and represent this on the left side of a sheet of paper with a small square.

  Step 2. Then, for each possible option, draw one line out from the square towards the right. Leave plenty of space between these lines. Write each option on it's line.

  Step 3. Then take the lines one at a time. At the end of the line, do you get a particular result, or is it uncertain or is there another decision to be made?.

  Step 4. If it is another decision, draw a square. If uncertain, a circle, and if a result, draw nothing (sometimes triangles are used for results).

  Step 5. Review each square and circle. For the squares (decisions), draw lines for the choices, marking them in as you go. For the circles (uncertainties) draw further lines for the possible outcomes.

  Step 6. Keep going until you have filled out the possibilities leading from your original decision.

Example:

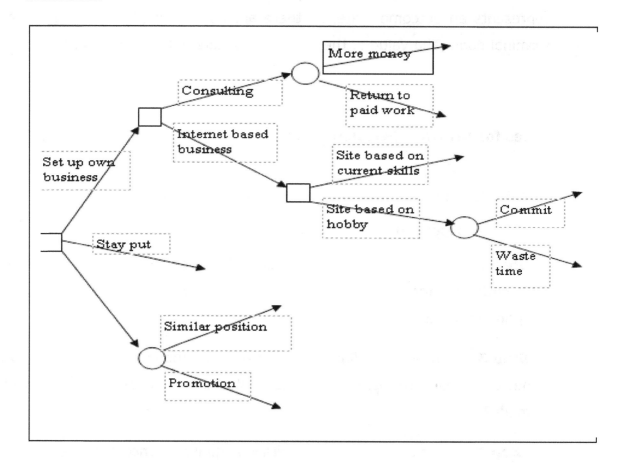

- **Evaluation**

Now it's time for decision tree analysis to work out which option is most valuable to you. First, estimate how much each option would be worth to you. (figures below)

Then review each circle/point of uncertainty. Here you determine the probability of each outcome. Make sure percentages add up to 100, or fractions amount to a total of 1. Your decision tree diagrams will now look something like this.

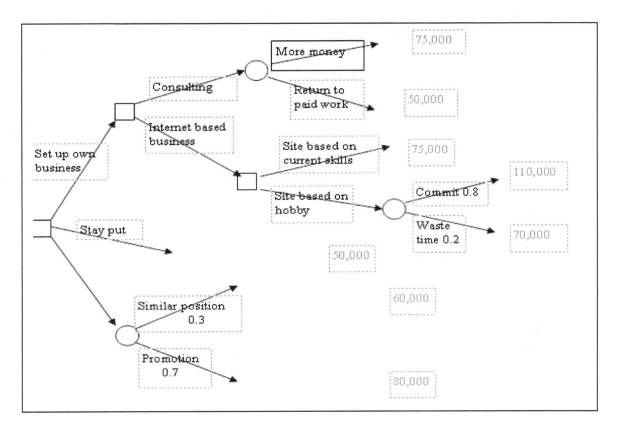

Example 2:

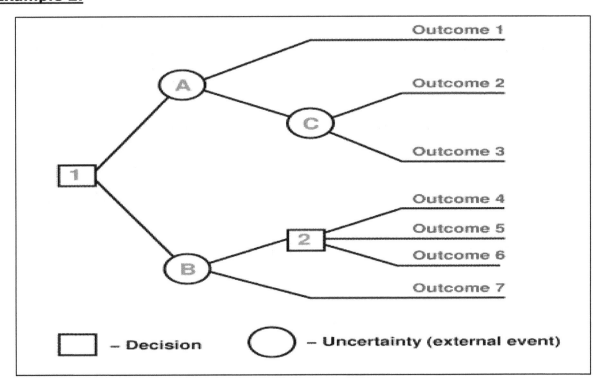

- **5 main Benefits of Decision Tree:**

1. The impact of possible future decisions:

A tree's branching and its spreading chain of events can clarify potential barriers, changes, and problems. The analyst can probe a variety of effects on his model tree by deliberately imposing faults and critical conditions to foresee their impact.

2. The impact of uncertainty on confidence:

Layout of the events in a tree structure makes more visible the alternatives that occur. Risk factor assignments or probabilities give better insight to and confidence in the future effects of a decision made in the present.

3. The impact of varying commitments of payoff:

Trying a variety of tentative objectives in a decision tree can reveal comparative advantages and disadvantages. These can be analyzed in a payoff table for criteria such as present or future profits. This validation procedure can frequently lead to restating the objective or selecting a new one.

4. The sequencing and interrelations of tasks and events:

The schematic display of starting events, secondary and terminating events allow for insights into input / output relationship and start/stop phasing as branching is extending into the future. Priorities can be established from the difficulties, complexities, and time requirements suggested by each path.

5. The measurement of risk:

Each path of the decision tree contains, in addition to the elements of the paths, and assigned risk factor. This is the estimated likelihood of occurrence of the terminal event in the path.

The decision trees satisfy a more complex need where a series of decisions are to be made simultaneously.

Barry Shore, has proposed the following procedure to solve a problem by the decision tree method.

(i) The problem is illustrated by developing tree diagram. Each course of action is represented by a separate emerging branch.

(ii) Each outcome for each course of action is assigned a probability, which is the most likely chance of that particular outcome occurring.

(iii) Determine the financial results of each outcome.

(iv) The expected value for each outcome is calculated and the alternative which will yield the highest expected value is chosen.

Decision trees depict future decision points and possible chance events. It adds to the confidence and accuracy of the decisions. Decision trees can be drawn to meet all sorts of situations.

Decision tree enables a planner: (a) to consider various courses of action; (b) to adding financial results to them (c) to modify these results by their probability; and (d) then to make comparisons.

Some decisions involve series of steps. Each step is not self-contained, but dependent on the outcome of the preceding step. For example, second step depending on outcome of second and so on. Thus with certainty mounting up with each step complexity comes in the problem's solutions.

Under such situations decision tree models provide an answer to such problems. Decision trees depict future decision points, and possible chance events - various uncertain things happening in future. It adds to the confidence and accuracy of the decisions. Decision trees can be drawn to meet all sorts of situations.

---------------------End------------------------

Topic 7. Data Dictionary

- ## Introduction of Data Dictionary

Data Dictionary is a collection of data describing the content, source, definition, structure, and business and derivation rules regarding the data within an organization. It is also called Metadata. Metadata is "data about the data", with examples being data types, lengths, scales, descriptions of the data elements and tables, entities, relationships, etc. Metadata data is stored in a repository to facilitate its accessibility. The metadata repository acts as a source of data to IT professionals in much the same manner as the Data Warehouse acts as a source of data to the business units within an organization.

Definition:-

- ## Data Dictionary:

"Data Dictionary is an analysis tool that primarily records the information content of data. It stores definitions of all data mentioned in DFD and in a process specification."

OR

"Data Dictionary is a central repository for database Meta data. Based on the above facts, it is evident that the Data Dictionary helps to increase sharing, integration and reusability of data."

- **Advantages of using a Data Dictionary:**

a. **Consistency:** Corporate data, repositories, etc. are only successful when they are consistently accessed and maintained within an organization, especially as that data crosses organizational boundaries. Data Dictionary helps to maintain the consistency of corporate data across organizations.

b. **Clarity:** Data Dictionary makes data clear and usable for the business user and the developer. This supports efficient and consistent use of the data by both the originators and the various users of the data regardless of what divisional organization they belong to. Often, non-standardized data is used because data elements are known within the originating organization without regard to other users outside their organization. The lack of clarity can cause an outside user to misunderstand the meaning, use, or domain of a data element and so, create an erroneous report affecting a management decision.

c. **Reusability:** Data Dictionary support consistency which is a key ingredient in the ability of one divisional organization to incorporate work that has already been designed, tested, and approved by the corporation for reuse into their own new development projects. Reinventing the wheel costs money and time. Reusability is enabled by application of standards to produce consistent parts for fitting into future work.

d. **Completeness:** Data Dictionary helps an analyst know when data is clear, complete, and defined by specifying what completeness means and the steps to develop a complete data structure. Incomplete data properties or descriptions tend to be improperly used and misunderstand of data. They can also cost extra time for a developer to make multiple phone calls to clarify and complete the information needed to use the data.

e. **Ease of Use for the Developer:** Having clear and complete definitions/descriptions for the data elements that the programmer must use to create the application functionality accurately minimizes costly development time.

- **What goes into Data Dictionary?**

  A data dictionary is organized into five sections:

  1. Data Elements

  2. Data Flows

  3. Data Stores

  4. Processes

  5. External Entities.

- **Formats of Data Dictionary (DD) ?**

  First of all data dictionary lists all the data elements, data flows, data stores and processes of the system under consideration. It then gives the details about each item listed in prescribed format.

  The data dictionary format is as bellow:

Sr. No.	Data Dictionary Item	Description
1.	Data Type	Data Element/Data Flow/Data Store
2.	Data Name	Name of the data Elements.
3.	Data Aliases	Alternate names used for the convenience of multiple users.
4.	Data Description	A short Description of data.
5.	Data Characteristics	Frequency of the use. Data length, Range of data values etc.
6.	Data Composition	Various data elements contained in a data store or data flow
7.	Data Control Information	Source or date of origin.
8.	Physical Location of Data	This is referred in terms of record, file or Database.

Note: At the making of time Data Dictionary all above every data dictionary item are not compulsory, only few one are sufficient.

- **Methodology for creating Data Dictionary (DD) ?**

So just what is a data dictionary and why have I learned to love them? System developers use a variety of tools when designing databases: pencil and paper, word processing, Microsoft Excel, or copying databases from similar systems. But none of these choices give you the data definition consistency forced by a data dictionary. Database management systems such as Visual FoxPro and Micros off SQL use data dictionaries to define the basic organization of a database. A data dictionary contains a list of all files in the database and the names and types of each field.

1. Data dictionaries don't contain any data from the database, only bookkeeping information for managing it. In the FoxPro environment, you create a table structure with MODIFY STRUCTURE, then build a database container consisting of those tables.

2. Similarly, you add tables to a SQL database, and fields to each table. In these systems, tables and data fields are dependent upon one another, which means a field such as CITY could be 25 bytes long in the Customer table and only 20 bytes long in the Vendor table.

3. Likewise, you could define a BALANCE field as a Numeric 12,2 in the customer table but as a Currency field in the Vendor table. This inconsistency causes confusion for designers, programmers, and users alike.

A way of creating and implementing a data dictionary as a design structure — you force consistency. As a methodology, a data dictionary manages a list of database tables and data fields (and their attributes), then specifies what fields to include in each table. This methodology could use index cards, as many programmers did in the old mainframe days, but is more commonly stored in small databases on a PC. When I create my data dictionary, I define and maintain tables and fields independently. The table list might include Customer, Vendor, and Invoice tables.

Example:

Table Layout: ReportCriteria		
Field Name	**Data Type**	**Description**
ItemID	AutoNumber	
ReportRef	Number	Foreign key to report table
FldName	Text	SQL field name
FldTitle	Text	Title (prompt) of field
FmtType	Text	(D=date/time,T=text,Y=yes/no,N=number,L=list,S=special)
Width	Number	Max character width (zero for default)
DefaultVal	Text	Default for field value
Sequence	Number	Position of field (low to high)
KeepWithPrior	Yes/No	Keep field together with prior field
Required	Yes/No	
Comparer	Text	SQL Comparer ("=", ">=", etc.) default to Like or = for num.
TheList	Text	List values if field is a drop-down-list, comma separated
FmtCodes	Text	Misc. formatting/validation codes

Table Layout: UserFields		
Field Name	**Data Type**	**Description**
userID	Number	
rptItemID	Number	Foreign key to ReportCriteria.ItemID
fldValue	Text	

Example 2:

	A	B	C	D
1	Table	Column	Datatype	Description
2	Categories	CategoryID	Int	Primary key
3	Categories	CategoryName	NVarChar (15)	Category name
4	Categories	Description	NText	Provided by marketing dept.
5	Categories	Picture	Image	Deprecated
6	CustomerCustomerD	CustomerID	NChar (5)	Link to Customers table
7	CustomerCustomerD	CustomerTypeI	NChar (10)	Link to CustomerDemographics
8	CustomerDemograp	CustomerTypeI	NChar (10)	Primary key
9	CustomerDemograp	CustomerDesc	NText	
10	Customers	CustomerID	NChar (5)	Primary key

----------------------End----------------------

Note:

Topic 8. Database Design

- **What is Database?**

As a part of system analysis and design, You try to find out requirements, system specification, user interface and Application development related issues etc. But everywhere you deal with amount of information, and that information is needed in different process or subsystem of whole application. This concept you treated as "DATA" and this data you need to maintain somewhere. That term you called as "Database". In other word collection of related data.

A database is simply a collection of organized information, usually as a set of related lists of similar entries. The data is often organized so that it is easily accessible. The following are examples of databases that we use often:

– Address book

– Dictionary

– Telephone book.

The portion of the real world relevant to the database is sometimes referred to as the **universe of discourse** or as the **database mini world**. Whatever it is called, it must be well understood by the designers of the database.

Definition:-

If you want to define the term database, then you can define this concept by various ways. Just see the following definition which will cover all basic and advanced concept of Database.

- **Database:**

    "A database is any collection of related data."

OR

"A database is a persistent, logically coherent collection of inherently meaningful data, relevant to some aspects of the real world."

- **Basics of Database**

➤ A database consists of a number of interrelated tables.
➤ Each table has a number of records which are used to represent real world objects.
  - For example, the police may have a record for each criminal that has ever been arrested (i.e., the "rap"-sheet)
➤ Each record has a number of fields which are data items used to specify a characteristic of the record.
➤ Examples of fields are:
  - name
  - employee number
  - address etc...

- **Who Need/ Uses the Database?**

Large databases are used all around the world. For example following,

Police :

• criminal records

Department of motor vehicles :

• driving history

• driving records

Banks

• all customers and their transactions

Government :

• statistics • election information • tax records etc.

- ## **Database Management System (DBMS) & RDBMS Concept:**

Database Management System (DBMS):

A Database Management System, or DBMS, is a computer application that allows you to work with databases on a computer.

• A database management system allows you to easily...

– Create/Delete tables

– Modify tables: (e.g., adding, deleting, editing and rearranging records, changing the table structure)

– Retrieve data from a table or a number of tables: (e.g., finding and displaying an individual record, answering queries (i.e., displaying specified field of records that satisfy a set of specified conditions)

– Create reports: (e.g., create formatted output of a list of specified fields of records that satisfy a set of specified conditions).

Relational Database Management System (RDBMS):

A database management system is a Relational Database Management System (RDBMS) if different tables are related to each other by common fields, so that information from several tables can be combined.

• For example, police detectives may cross reference phone records or driving records to make a connection or relationship between two or more criminals.

- ## **There are 3 basic things that you do with a DBMS:**

– **Design:** You must first create the database by defining the tables which specifies what is to be stored.

– **Data Entry:** Once the tables have been created, someone has to enter ALL the data (i.e., information)

– **Fire Queries:** Once we have the database with data entered, we can then ask questions (also known as Queries) about the data.

- **Who Interacts with a DBMS?**

Many different individuals are involved with a database management system over its life:

• Systems analysts

• Database designers

• Database administrators

• Application developers

• Users

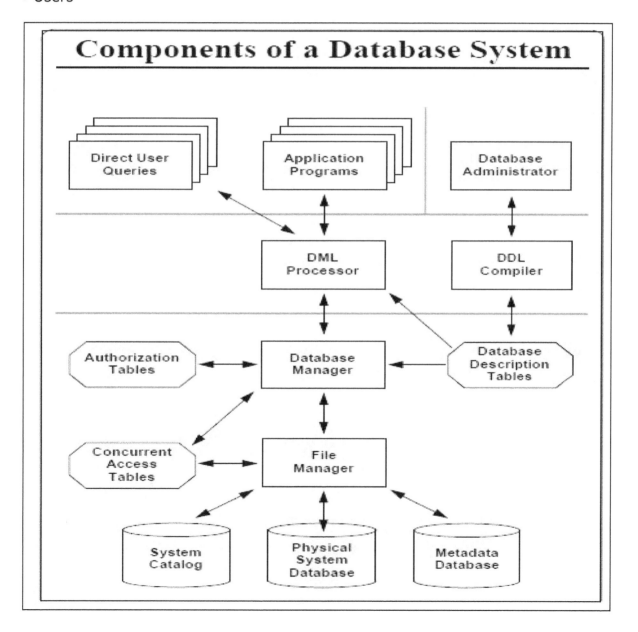

- **Introduction Of Database Design:**

When designing a database, the goals must be clearly defined in order to ensure that the development process runs smooth from phase to phase, that the effort is cost-effective, and that a complete and accurate model is derived. The primary goal of the end product, the completed database, must be a database that meets the data storage needs of the customer.

It is important to identify the short-term and long-term goals, the services or products provided the different types of business processes, the types of users who perform these processes, the expectancy of the new database, and the customer's perception of the database. How will the new database benefit the end user? How will the new database evolve in both the near future and distant future? Are there manual processes that can be automated? What existing automated processes can be refined? These are just a few considerations that should be taken when defining design goals for a new database.

- **What is a Database Design?**

Webster's dictionary uses the following phrases to define the term design:
- "To prepare the preliminary plans or sketch for"
- "To intend for a definite purpose"
- "The combination of details or features of something constructed"
- "To plan and fashion artistically or skillfully"
- "Adaptation of means to a preconceived end"

Each of Webster's definitions can be used to explain the purpose of database design and the events that should take place during database design.

"To prepare the preliminary plans or sketch for" implies that there is more work in database design than what is obvious on the surface.

Before the actual design of the database occurs, there is much planning involved. Before any design effort commences, the "definite purpose" of the database should be clearly defined. The problems of the legacy database or manual processes should be addressed, and solutions are proposed. There should not be any questions as to the purpose of the proposed database. Many "details and features" are involved during the design of any database. Once the purpose of the database has been established, the design team should study all of the details and features that comprise the business. These details and features, once gathered and often "sketched," are eventually formatted into a database structure using a predetermined database model.

During the actual design of the database, these details and features are "fashioned artistically and skillfully" into a database model, which will most likely be modified numerous times before the design process is complete.

"Adaptation of means to a preconceived end" is an excellent phrase used to describe the activities of database designers in many situations. The designers must be able to adapt the phases and tasks in database design to roll with the changes and meet the customer's needs. Often, the designers find that the customer's needs for a database are refined throughout the design process, or even changed drastically. The designers should be able to receive further requests that affect the functionality of the database, and be able to adapt the steps taken during the different phases of design if necessary to integrate any changes proposed.

- **Phases of Database Design:**

Three very basic phases of database design exist, which are as follows,:
- ➢ **Requirements Gathering:**
- ➢ **Data Modeling:**
- ➢ **Database Design & Normalization:**

• Requirements gathering:-

It is the process of conducting meetings and/or interviews with customers, end users, and other individuals in the company to establish the requirements for the proposed database. Requirements involve, but are not limited to, the following information:

How the business does business?

Business rules and processes.

Information about the current database being used.

Future needs of the business as related to the database.

• Data modeling:-

It is the process of visually representing the data for a business, and then eventually converting the business model into a data model. The data model generated is used to ultimately create the tables, views, and other objects that comprise the database.

• Database design and normalization:-

It is a phase in which the business model (logical model) is converted into a physical model (tables). Also part of design is normalization, or the reduction or elimination of data redundancy. Usually, the lines between these three phases are foggy, and might not seem clearly defined because the requirements of every business and the skill sets of individuals within every company, vary.

Database Design Planning is next phase where all schedule are made regarding to designing the database.

- **Importance of Database Design:**

Now that the concept of database design has been thoroughly defined, it is imperative to understand the importance of the design process. Although the importance of design might seem obvious, just remember that design seems obvious to most people until they are submersed into a major project with intense deadlines and little direction. Before starting, the design team must step back, take a deep breath, and plan the steps of the design process carefully before lunging foreword uncontrollably. It is important that the database design project gets off to a good, clean start with a solid plan.

The main reason good database design is so important is that organization is promoted.

The designers have more control over the design, implementation, and management of any project, if the project is well thought out. Because the database design's goal is to completely capture all a business' data storage needs, its product should be an accurate and easy-to-use database that performs well.

Suppose that the design of a database has been well thought out, and the final database is complete in that it entails all business processes, rules, and has an application interface that is easy for the customer to use.

In a database such as this, data is easily retrieved and modified. Also from the user perspective, the actual design of the database is transparent as the end user works with the application. From the database administration standpoint, maintenance on the database is simplified and easy to perform.

The database itself will ensure data integrity and adherence to business rules.

Now, consider a database that has been thrown together fiercely with little thought during initial design. All business rules might not have been captured. Data integrity might not be fully implemented because all rules have not been captured. Why are business rules and processes missing? There are missing elements because there was not clear direction on how to proceed with the design phase. Without a well-thought out design plan, customers and users were not interviewed thoroughly enough, and feedback sessions might not have been conducted with the end user and customer to ensure that all business elements were completely captured. Now, the company is stuck with a database that isn't fully functional and might involve additional manual processes to ensure data accuracy and consistency, which defeats the purpose of database planning and design. A situation such as this is frustrating for management, the technical team, and especially the customer.

- **Understanding the Database Design Process:**

  - **The Importance of Good Database Design**

    1. A good database design is crucial for a high-performance application, just as an aerodynamic body is important to a race car. If the car doesn't have smooth lines, it will produce drag and go slower.

    2. Without optimized relationships, your database won't perform as efficiently as possible. Thinking about relationships and database efficiency is part of *normalization.*

    3. Beyond the issue of performance is the issue of maintenance—your database should be easy to maintain. This includes storing only a limited amount (if any) of repetitive data.

    4. If you have a lot of repetitive data and one instance of that data undergoes a change (such as a name change), that change has to be made

for all occurrences of the data. To eliminate duplication and enhance your ability to maintain the data, you might create a table of possible values and use a key to refer to the value. That way, if the value changes names, the change occurs only once—in the master table. The reference remains the same throughout other tables.

- **Table Design Considerations**

The vast majority of the work in identifying and defining database tables is done during logical modeling and design of the entities from which physical table structures are derived. During logical design, you identify and capture in a logical model the entities (things of significance) in the real-world system you need to model through your database and the applications that utilize it. Examples of entities would be students, customers, employees, products, and orders.

Much of logical database design revolves around identifying the entities in the system and then identifying the descriptive facts about these entities that will be included as attributes. Attributes of a student entity might be last name, first name, middle initial, address, date of birth, social security number, and so on. During logical design of relational databases, many of the initial entities identified in the data model will be further broken up into two or more additional entities, each with fewer attributes, by iteratively applying a set of logical rules to the entities in a process called *normalization*.

Logical entities from the logical design phase are transformed into tables. The biggest difference between entities and tables is that entities are logical structures only. They represent a class of items the database must logically model but do not contain any specific examples or instances of that class. Entities have no data rows. Tables are still logical structures, but they contain many rows of data and are tied closely to the physical files utilized by the RDBMS to actually store the data on the database's host computer.

Data for a particular table will be stored in a particular physical data file or combination of physical data files that the table is associated with in a manner dependent on the particular RDBMS being used. Some entities will come through the transformation design process to tables relatively unchanged. In such cases, the structure of the table and its columns will look almost exactly like the logical entity and its attributes from which the table is derived. The notable addition to even those tables that are relatively unchanged will likely be the inclusion of foreign key columns in the table needed as part of the underpinnings for referential integrity constraints within the database.

- ## Referential Integrity in Table Design

Referential integrity is the glue that binds the tables of a database together. One of the columns of a table or a combination of table columns in a row will make up a unique identifier or primary key for each and every row in the table. In addition, the primary key column (or columns) or other non-key columns from the parent table (the "one" side in a one-to-many relationship or one of the "one" sides in the occasional one-to-one relationship) is propagated to the structure of the child table as a foreign key column, and joins between the two tables are generally done based on equality of the parent and child key relationship columns. In addition to the foreign key relationship being the basis for joins, prior to adding a row to the child table, the RDBMS will check the parent table column that the foreign key column of the child table refers to in order to ensure that the parent table column has a row that includes the specific foreign key column value in the row you're trying to add in the new child table row. If the parent table doesn't have that exact value in the column that the child foreign key refers to, the proposed new row in the child table will be rejected.

- **Importance of the Logical Model in Table Design**

A table's logical structure (column names, column data types, and column sizes) is derived from the logical entity structures defined during logical database design as you build an entity relationship diagram (ERD). Logical design produces an unconstrained logical data model of an enterprise's data requirements. Table structures are those unconstrained entity structures transformed with the consideration of the physical database design, such as with the association between data storage and application performance. The ERD entities are transformed into the logical structure for the tables of a relational database. Entity attributes will become table columns. Entity unique identifiers will become table primary keys. Entity domains will become table data constraints. Entity relationships will become table primary and foreign key referential integrity constraints.

Logical database entity design is not constrained by concerns for physical performance. Its purpose is to correctly model the data structure requirements for the business processes the database must support and to do away with data redundancy and other data structure errors. Normalization does away with redundant data columns. A particular data column is stored in a single table to simplify updates and prevent errors when one table gets updated and the other doesn't. Derived data columns that are the result of calculations on other columns or concatenations of other columns are also not allowed in a normalized structure. The normalization process produces many tables with relatively few columns.

The benefits of a well-planned and designed database are numerous, and it stands to reason that the more work you do up front, the less you'll have to do later. A really bad time for a database redesign is after the public launch of the application using it—although it does happen, and the results are costly.
So, before you even start coding an application, spend a lot of time designing your database.

- **Types of Table Relationships**

Table relationships come in several forms:

. *One-to-one relationships*

. *One-to-many relationships*

. *Many-to-many relationships*

For example, suppose that you have a table called employees that contains each person's Social Security number, name, and the department in which he or she works. Suppose that you also have a separate table called departments, containing the list of all available departments, made up of a Department ID and a name. In the employees table, the Department ID field matches an ID found in the departments table. You can see this type of relationship in following figure. The PK next to the field name indicates the primary key for the table.

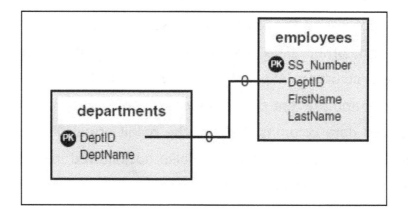

> ## One-to-One Relationships

In a one-to-one relationship, a key appears only once in a related table. The employees and departments tables do not have a one-to-one relationship because many employees undoubtedly belong to the same department. A one-to-one relationship exists, for example, if each employee is assigned one computer within a company. Following figure shows the one-to-one relationship of employees to computers.

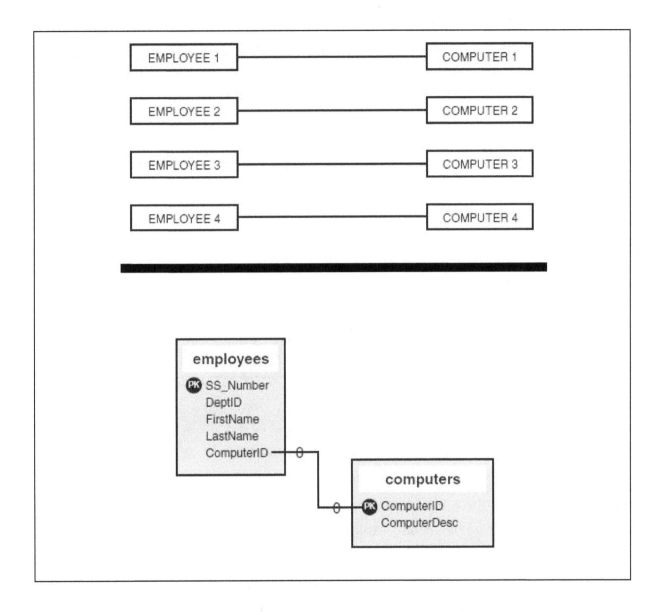

➤ One-to-Many Relationships

The one-to-many relationship is the most common type of relationship. In a one-to-many relationship, keys from one table appear multiple times in a related table. The example shown in above first Figure, indicating a connection between employees and departments, illustrates a one-to-many relationship. A real-world example would be an organizational chart of the department, as shown in Following Figure.

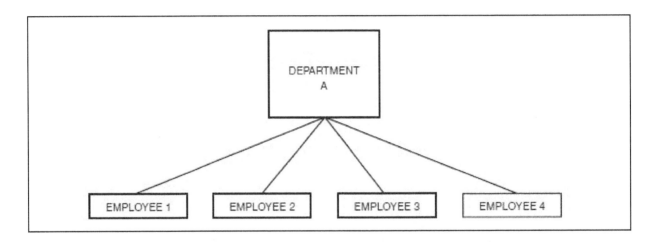

➤ Many-to-Many Relationships

The many-to-many relationship often causes problems in practical examples of normalized databases, so much so that it is common to simply break many-to-many relationships into a series of one-to-many relationships. In a many-to-many relationship, the key value of one table can appear many times in a related table. So far, it sounds like a one-to-many relationship, but here's the curveball: The opposite is also true, meaning that the primary key from that second table can also appear many times in the first table.

Think of such a relationship this way, using the example of students and classes: A student has an ID and a name. A class has an ID and a name. A student usually takes more than one class at a time, and a class always contains more than one student, as you can see in next Figure.

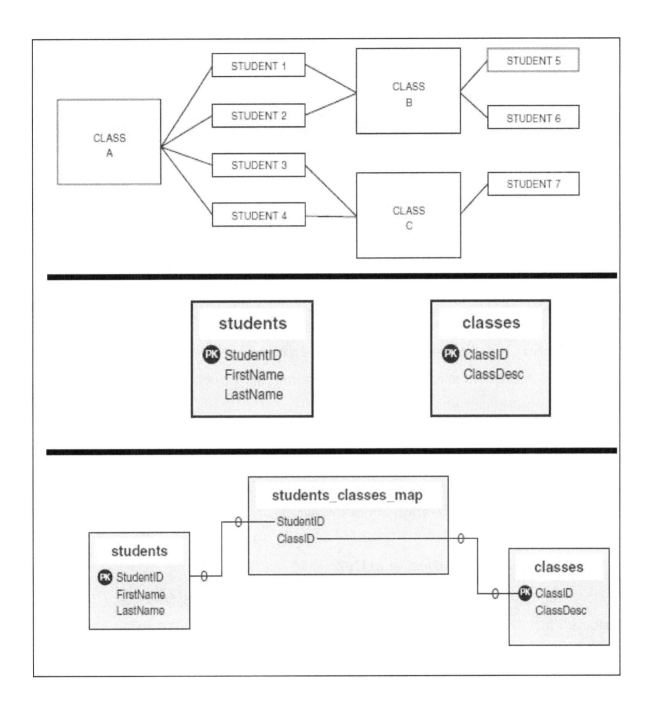

As you can see, this sort of relationship doesn't present an easy method for relating tables. Your tables could look like above Figure, seemingly unrelated. To make the theoretical many-to-many relationship, you would create an intermediate table, one that sits between the two tables and essentially maps them together. You might build such a table similar to the one.

• Normalization

Normalization is simply a set of rules that will ultimately make your life easier when you're acting as a database administrator. It's the art of organizing your database in such a way that your tables relate where appropriate and are flexible for future growth. The sets of rules used in normalization are called **normal forms**. If your database design follows the first set of rules, it's considered in the **first normal form**. If the first three sets of rules of normalization are followed, your database is said to be in the **third normal form**.

➤ Database Tables and Normalization

Normalization is a process for assigning attributes to entities. It reduces data redundancies and helps eliminate the data anomalies. Normalization works through a series of stages called normal forms:

First normal form (1NF)

Second normal form (2NF)

Third normal form (3NF)

The highest level of normalization is not always desirable.

➤ What is Normalization exactly?

GOLDEN RULE OF NORMALIZATION: Enter The Minimum Data Necessary, Avoiding Duplicate Entry Of Information, With Minimum Risks To Data Integrity.

Goals Of Normalization:

1. **Eliminate Redundancies Caused By:**
   Fields Repeated Within A File
   Fields Not Directly Describing The Key Entity
   Fields Derived From Other Fields
2. **Avoid Anomalies In Updating (Adding, Editing,Deleting)**
3. **Represent Accurately The Items Being Modeled**
4. **Simplify Maintenance And Retrieval of Info**

- ## The Need for Normalization

In Case of a Construction Company

Building project -- Project number, Name, Employees assigned to the project.

Employee -- Employee number, Name, Job classification

The company charges its clients by billing the hours spent on each project. The hourly billing rate is dependent on the employee's position.

- ## Normalization Benefits

1. Facilitates data integration.
2. Reduces data redundancy.
3. Provides a robust architecture for retrieving and maintaining data.
4. Compliments data modeling.
5. Reduces the chances of data anomalies occurring.

- ## Start for Doing Normalization:

Consider the students-and-courses database, assume that you have the following fields in your flat table:

. **StudentName**—The name of the student.

. **CourseID1**—The ID of the first course taken by the student.

. **CourseDescription1**—The description of the first course taken by the student.

. **CourseInstructor1**—The instructor of the first course taken by the student.

. **CourseID2**—The ID of the second course taken by the student.

. **CourseDescription2**—The description of the second course taken by the student.

. **CourseInstructor2**—The instructor of the second course taken by the student.

. Repeat CourseID, CourseDescription, and CourseInstructor columns many more times to account for all the classes students can take during their academic career.

With what you've learned so far, you should be able to identify the first problem area: CourseID, CourseDescription, and CourseInstructor columns are repeated groups.

Eliminating redundancy is the first step in normalization, so next you'll take this flat table to first normal form. If your table remained in its flat format, you could have a lot of unclaimed space and a lot of space being used unnecessarily—not an efficient table design.

First Normal Form (1NF)

The rules for the first normal form are as follows:

. ***Eliminate repeating information.***

. ***Create separate tables for related data.***

If you think about the flat table design with many repeated sets of fields for the students-and-courses database, you can identify two distinct topics: students and courses. Taking your students-and-courses database to the first normal form would mean that you create two tables: one for students and one for courses, as shown in following Figure.

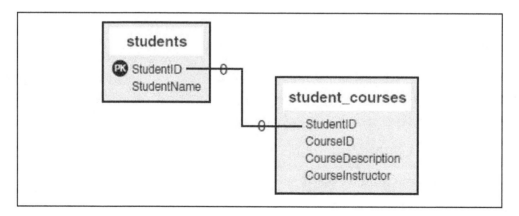

Your two tables now represent a one-to-many relationship of one student to many courses. Students can take as many courses as they want and are not limited to the number of CourseID/CourseDescription/CourseInstructor groupings that existed in the flat table.

The next step is to put the tables into second normal form.

Second Normal Form (2NF)

The rule for the second normal form is as follows:

No non-key attributes depend on a portion of the primary key.

In plain English, this means that if fields in your table are not entirely related to a primary key, you have more work to do. In the students-and-courses example, you need to break out the courses into their own table and modify the students_courses table.

CourseID, CourseDescription, and CourseInstructor can become a table called courses with a primary key of CourseID. The students_courses table should then just contain two fields: StudentID and CourseID. You can see this new design in following Figure:

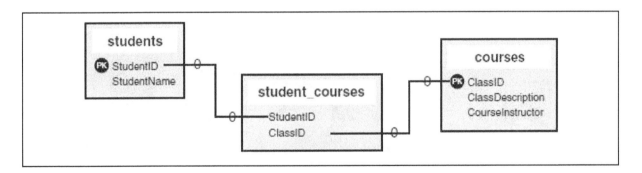

This structure should look familiar to you as a many-to-many relationship using an intermediary mapping table. The third normal form is the last form you'll look at, and you'll find it's just as simple to understand as the first two.

Third Normal Form (3NF)

The rule for the third normal form is as follows:

No attributes depend on other non-key attributes.

This rule simply means that you need to look at your tables and see whether you have more fields that can be broken down further and that aren't dependent on a key. Think about removing repeated data and you'll find your answer: instructors. Inevitably, an instructor will teach more than one class. However, CourseInstructor is not a key of any sort. So, if you break out this information and create a separate table purely for the sake of efficiency and maintenance (as shown in bellow Figure), that's the third normal form.

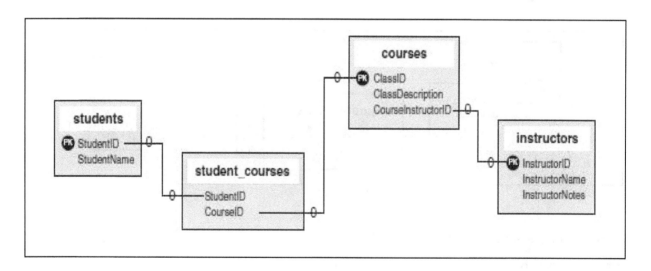

Third normal form is usually adequate for removing redundancy and allowing for flexibility and growth. The next section will give you some pointers for the thought process involved in database design and where it fits in the overall design process of your application.

-----------------------**End**-------------------------

Topic 9. Software Requirement Specification (S.R.S)

- **Introduction of SRS (Software Requirement Specification)**

The SRS document is known as black-box specification:

– The system is considered as a black box whose internal details are not known.

– Only its visible external (i.e. input/output) behavior is documented.

SRS document concentrates on:

– What needs to be done?

– Carefully avoids the solution ("how to do") aspects.

– The SRS document serves as a contract between development team and the customer.

– Should be carefully written.

The requirements at this stage:

– written using end-user terminology.

If necessary:

– later a formal requirement specification may be developed from it.

Definition:-

- **Software Requirement Specification (S.R.S):**

"The SRS is a document that completely describes what the proposed software should do without describing how the software will do it."

OR

"SRS document is a contract between the development team and the customer."

OR

"SRS is the medium through which the client and the user needs are accurately specified; indeed SRS forms the basis of software development."

- **Understanding the Software Requirement Specification:**

  ➤ Purpose of SRS is as follows:

  1. It is Communication between the Customer, Analyst, system developers, maintainers etc.

  2. SRS is contract between Purchaser and Supplier.

  3. SRS is used for Firm foundation for the design phase.

  4. SRS support system testing activities.

  5. SRS support project management and control.

  6. SRS controlling the evolution of the system.

  ➤ Software Requirements Specification (SRS) Defines the customer's requirements in terms of :
  - Function
  - Performance
  - External interfaces
  - Design constraints

  ➤ What is not included in an SRS?
  - Project requirements.
  - Cost, delivery schedules, staffing, reporting procedures.
  - Design solutions.
  - partitioning of SW into modules, choosing data structures.
  - Product assurance plans.
  - Quality Assurance procedures, Configuration Management procedures, verification & Validation procedures.

• Benefits of SRS

1. Forces the users to consider their specific requirements carefully .
2. Enhances communication between the Purchaser and System developers.
3. Provides a firm foundation for the system design phase.
4. Enables planning of validation, verification, and acceptance procedures.
5. Enables project planning eg. estimates of cost and time, resource scheduling.
6. Usable during maintenance phase.

• Software Requirements & Types of Requirements:

Definition:-

• Software Requirements:

"A condition of capability needed by a user to solve a problem or achieve an objective."

OR

"A condition or a capability that must be met on possessed by a system to satisfy a contract, standard, specification or other formally imposed document."

• Types of Requirements

1. Functional requirements.
2. Non functional requirements.
   2.1 Performance requirements.
   2.2 Interface requirements.
   2.3 Design constraints.
   2.4 Other requirements.

➢ Functional Requirements:

The functional Requirements consist of,

1. Transformations (inputs, processing, outputs)
2. Requirements for sequencing and parallelism (dynamic requirements)
3. Data
4. Inputs and Outputs
   - Stored data
   - Transient data
5. Exception handling
6. Nature of function: Mandatory/ Desirable/
       Optional / Volatile / Stable

➢ Performance Requirements:

The Performance Requirements consist of,

1. Capacity
   - no. of simultaneous users, processing requirements for normal and
     peak loads, static storage capacity, spare capacity
2. Response time
3. System priorities for users and functions
4. System efficiency
5. Availability
6. Fault recovery

Note: - *All these requirements should be stated in measurable terms so that they can be verified. A requirement is verifiable if and only if there exists some finite cost effective process with which a person or machine can check that the SW meets the requirement.*

> **External Interface Requirements:**

The Interface Requirements consist of,

1. User interfaces
   - eg. if display terminal used, specify required screen formats, menus, report layouts, function keys.
2. Hardware interfaces
   - characteristics of the interface between the SW product and HW components of the system.
3. Software interfaces.
4. Specify the use of other SW products eg. OS, DBMS, other SW packages.

> **Design Constraints:**

1. Software design constraints
   - Standards for design, coding, naming, etc.
   - SW interfaces (to OS, DBMS, other SW)
   - use a specific application package.
   - Constraints on program size, data size etc.
2. Hardware design constraints
   - Specific type of HW, reliability requirements.
   - Hardware interfaces.
   - Requirements for spare capacity or spare performance.
3. User-interface design constraints
   - Features of operator/user with details of working environment.
   - Any special features required.

> Other Requirements:

The other requirement is an last part of Requirement type, which consist of following things:

1. Security
2. Safety
3. Environmental
4. Reusability
5. Training

- ## Structure of S.R.S. Defined by IEEE

Sr. No.	SRS Content		
1.	**Introduction**		
	1.1	Overview	
	1.2	Purpose	
	1.3	Scope	
	1.4	Definitions, Acronyms and Abbreviations	
	1.5	References	
2.	**Overall Description**		
	2.1	Product Perspective	
	2.2	Product Functions	
	2.3	User Characteristics	
	2.4	General Constraints	
	2.5	Assumptions and Dependencies	
3.	**Specific Requirements**		
	3.1	**External Interface Requirements**	
	3.1.1		User Interfaces
	3.1.2		Hardware Interfaces
	3.1.3		Software Interfaces
	3.1.4		Communication Interfaces
	3.2	**Functional Requirements**	
	3.2.1		Mode 1 to Mode n Functional Requirements
	3.3	**Performance Requirements**	
4.	**Design Constraints**		
5.	**Software System Attributes**		
6.	**Other Requirements**		
7.	**Supporting Information**		

1] Introduction:

1.1 Overview:

In terms of introduction we have to explain flow of existing system in short summary where name of system should reflect like: Library Management System. In detail we have write every transaction in the system.

In the section of introduction, overview of the product (application) is first point which will describe what the rest of the SRS contains. And explain the how the SRS is organized? Following things should be covered in the overview:

1. What is the proposed system?
2. Who are the users of proposed system?
3. What Requirements will be fulfilling in proposed system?
4. Is the system will fulfill needs & features on high level?

1.2 Purpose:

In the purpose we have to specify the purpose of the particular SRS and specify the intended audience for the SRS. The purpose of SRS document should explain external behavior of the proposed system. The purpose should focus on operations, interfaces, performance, quality assurance requirements and the design constraints.

1.3 Scope:

The scope of SRS should cover following points:

1. Identify the Software products to be produced by name
2. Explain what the Software product will do, and if necessary, what it will not do?
3. Describe the application of the SW being specified. ie.benefits, objectives, goals as precisely as possible

1.4 Definitions, Acronyms and Abbreviations:

List out the various Definitions, Acronyms and Abbreviations terms present in the proposed system. At the time of listing all this term consider database used for making proposed system as well as short forms used in preparing SRS etc. Every acronyms and abbreviations should list out sequentially.

Eg: PIN - Personal Identification Number

1.5 References:

It includes the references cited in the document and any definitions that are used. All Journal, documents and web references listing here.

Eg: http://www.ieee.org/index.html

2] Overall Description:

2.1 Product Perspective:

In the product perspective state whether the product is independent and totally self contained. If the product is component of a larger system then:

1. Describe the functions of each component of the larger system and identify interfaces.

2. Overview of the principal external interfaces of this product.

3. Overview of HW and peripheral equipment to be used.

Give a block diagram showing the major components of the product, interconnections, and external interfaces.

2.2 Product Function:

In SRS document as a part of product function provide a summary of functions the software will perform. The functions should be organized in such a way that they are understandable by the user.

2.3 User Characteristics:

Here we have to describe the general characteristics of the eventual users of the product. (Such as educational level, experience and technical expertise)

2.4 General Constraints:

The general constraints include following:

1. Regulatory policies.
2. Hardware limitations.
3. Interfaces to other applications.
4. Parallel operation.
5. Audit functions.
6. Control functions.
7. Criticality of the application.
8. Safety and security considerations.

2.5 Assumptions and dependencies:

State the basic needs which will be helpful for use proposed system. It also includes primary assumptions, required sources, Communication interface, and user interaction.

Eg. Internet connection, English as communication language etc.

3] Specific Requirement:

3.1 External Interface Requirements:

One of the most important part of SRS, where describes the sources or platform required for running proposed system or software or application.

It include following things:

1. Hardware interfaces.

2. Software interfaces.

3. Communications interfaces.

4. Other requirements.

5. Database: frequency of use, accessing capabilities, Static and dynamic organization, retention requirements for data.

6. Operations: periods of interactive and unattended operations, backup, recovery operations.

7. Site adaptation requirements.

3.2 Functional Requirements:

In the functional requirements section the functional capabilities of the system are described. In the organization the functional capabilities for all the modes of operation of the software must be there. For each functional requirement the required inputs, desired outputs and processing requirements will have to be specified. For the inputs, the source of the inputs, the units of measure, valid ranges, accuracies etc. have to be specified.

For specifying the processing and operations that need to be performed on the input data and any intermediate data produced should be specified. This includes validity checks on inputs, sequence of operations response to abnormal conditions and methods that must be used in processing to transform the inputs into corresponding outputs. No algorithms are generally specified.

In the performance section specify both static and dynamic requirements. All factors that constrain the system design are described in the performance constrain section.

4] Design Constraints:

In the Design Constraints section following constraints should be covered:

➢ SW design constraints
    1. Standards for design, coding, naming, etc.
    2. Software interfaces (to OS, DBMS, other Software)
    3. Use a specific application package
    4. Constraints on program size, data size etc.

➢ HW design constraints
    1. Specific type of HW, reliability requirements
    2. Hardware interfaces
    3. Requirements for spare capacity or spare Performance

➢ User-interface design constraints
    1. Features of operator/user with details of working environment
    2. Any special features required.

5] Software System Attributes:

In this section of SRS discuss how the system problem are solved?, how software provide more security in terms of database. List out various parameter which will focus on system quality/software/application. This attributes are as follows:
    1. Reliability
    2. Availability
    3. Security
    4. Maintainability
    5. Portability
    6. Performance

6] Other Requirements:

Any requirements not covered under functional requirement section are covered under the other requirements section. The information written here in forms of,

1. Licensing Requirements.
2. Applicable Standards
3. EULA (End user License Agreement)

6] Supporting Information:

This is last section of an SRS where we have to include supporting information for making SRS as well as software. In other words before accepting the system, the developer must be demonstrating that the system works on the number of stock data, product, and quantity specification. The developer will have to show through test cases that all conditions are satisfied.

Characteristics of a Good SRS

A good SRS contains following characteristics:

1. Unambiguous
2. Complete
3. Verifiable
4. Consistent
5. Modifiable
6. Traceable
7. Usable during the Operation and Maintenance phase

SRS Summary

- **SRS Review**

1. Formal Review done by Users, Developers, Managers, Operations personnel
2. To verify that SRS confirms to the actual user requirements
3. To detect defects early and correct them.
4. Review typically done using checklists.

- **Sample SRS Checklist**

1. Are all HW resources defined?
2. Have response times been specified for functions?
3. Have all the HW, external SW and data interfaces been defined?
4. Is each requirement testable?
5. Is the initial state of the system defined?
6. Are the responses to exceptional conditions specified?
7. Are possible future modifications specified?

----------------------**End**-------------------------

Note:

Topic 10. CASE STUDIES BASED ON ERD

❖ Tips to remember at the time of drawing E.R.D. :

→ Entity should not be on hanging mode or hanged.

→ In ERD there should be a complete flow.

→ For an entity show at least key attributes (means those attribute having primary key and foreign key).

→ The complete ERD moves from left to right or top to bottom direction.

→ Try to use specialization whenever necessary.

→ Depict the relationship (1-1, 1-m, m-1,m-m).

→ Don't show directional arrow lines in the flow of ERD.

→ When you are consider any entity it means that, there is table exists in the database for that entity.

→ ERD should be cleared and easy to understand. Also it will cover all the flow of the system.

❖ Tricks to Solve Case (Draw ERD for given Case/System) :

→ Read Case carefully and try to understand system in detail.

→ Analyze & find out every sequence of flow in the system.

→ Find out every entity & relationship exists between then with reference to database.

Case I: Draw ERD for Medical Expert System

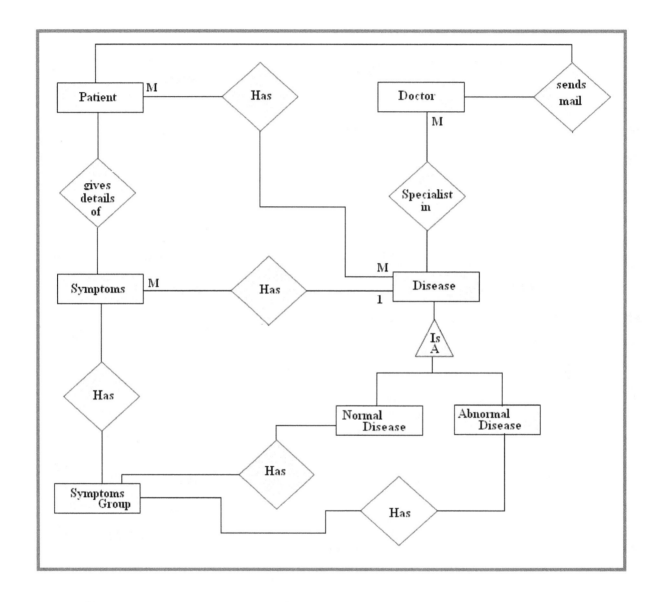

Case II: Draw ERD for Learning License Test System

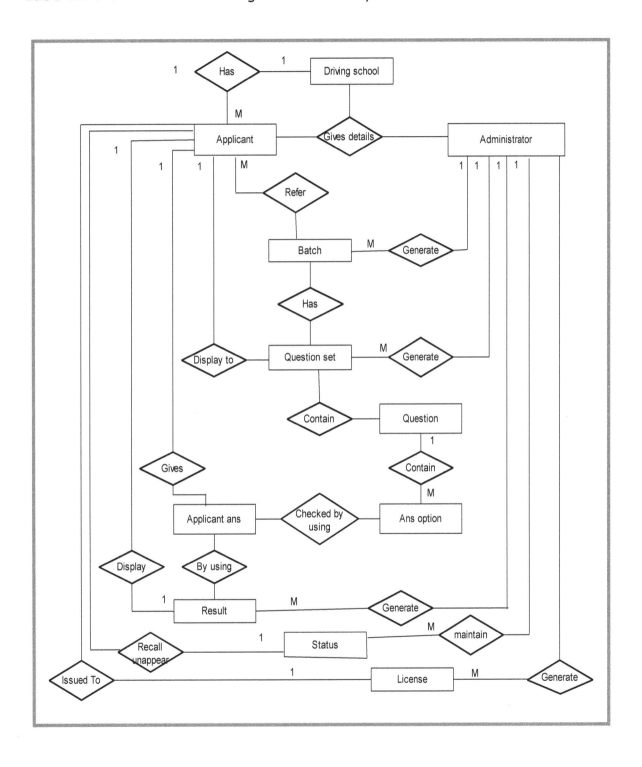

Case III: Draw ERD for Logistic Monitor System

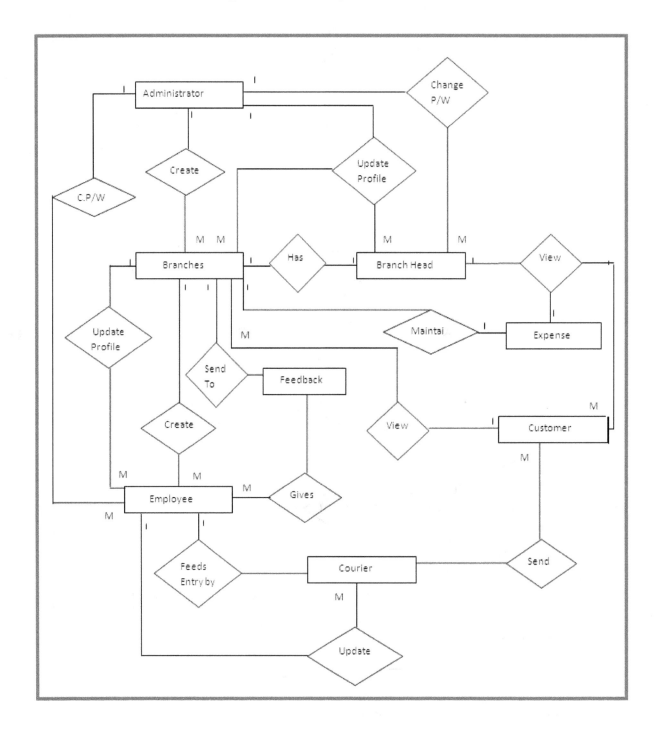

Case IV: Draw ERD for Institute Marketing Management System

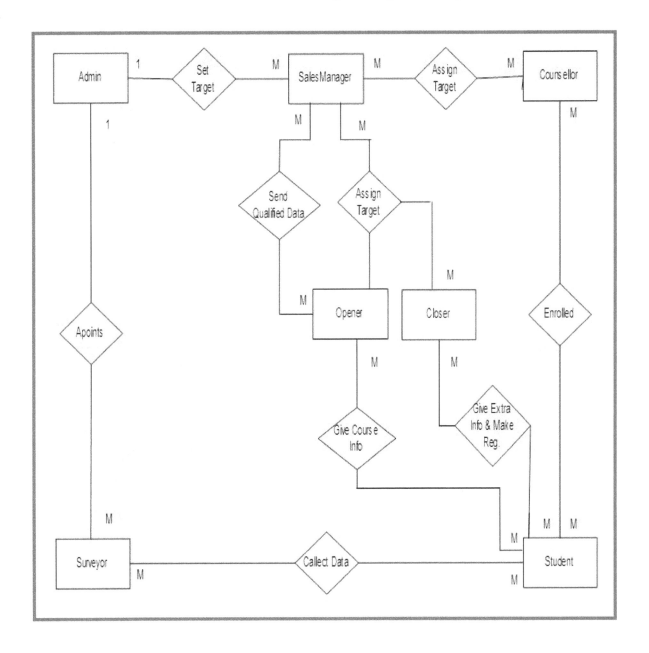

Case V: Draw ERD for Merit Track System (Online Exam System)

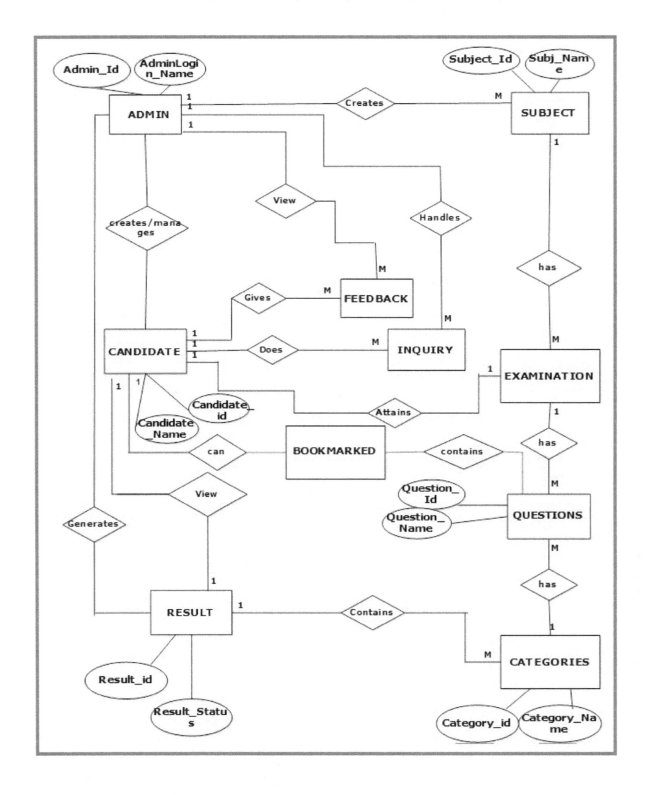

Case VI: Draw ERD for Electrical Management System for Contractor

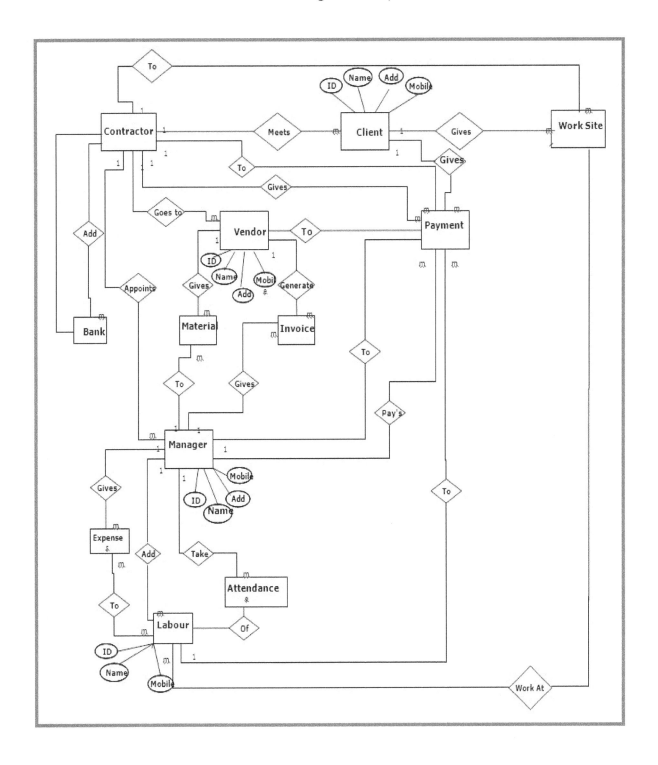

Case VII: Draw ERD for E-Farming(System is useful for farmer using online portal)

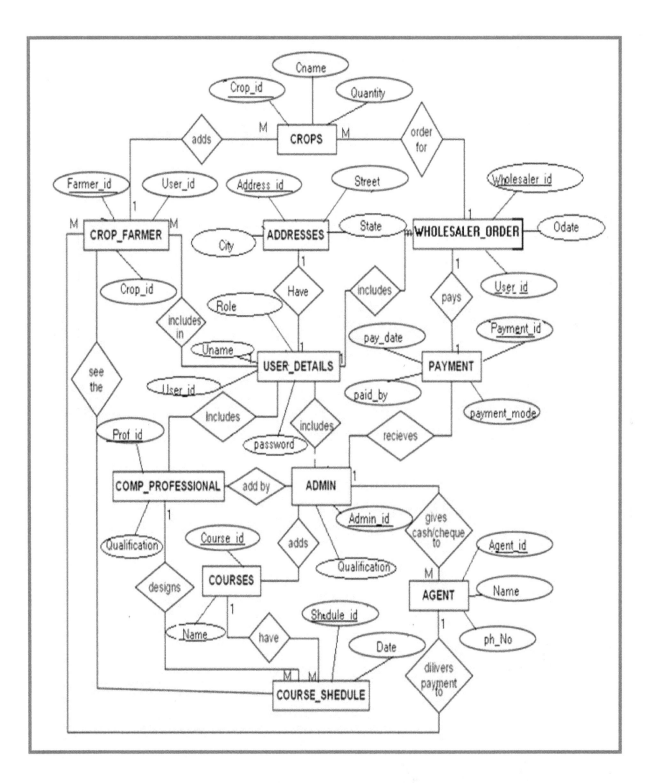

Topic 11. CASE STUDIES BASED ON FDD

❖ Tips to remember at the time of drawing F.D.D. :

➔ Consider all subsystem in your main system or application.

➔ Analyze all subsystem & show it into FDD as a subparts or subprocesses.

➔ For an entity show at least key attributes (means those attribute having primary key and foreign key).

➔ Follow the top to bottom approach while drawing FDD.

➔ Cover all events or task associated with subprocesses and user in FDD.

➔ Give proper numbering to each level of decomposition.

❖ Tricks to Solve Case (Draw FDD for given Case/System) :

➔ Read Case carefully and try to understand system in detail.

➔ Analyze & find out every subsystem or subprocess in the system.

➔ Find out every action or events in every subsystem.

Case I: Draw FDD for Medical Expert System

The Medical Expert System is made up of different subsystems like registration, login, questionnaires, diagnosis, mail & report generation. So the final FDD is as follows:

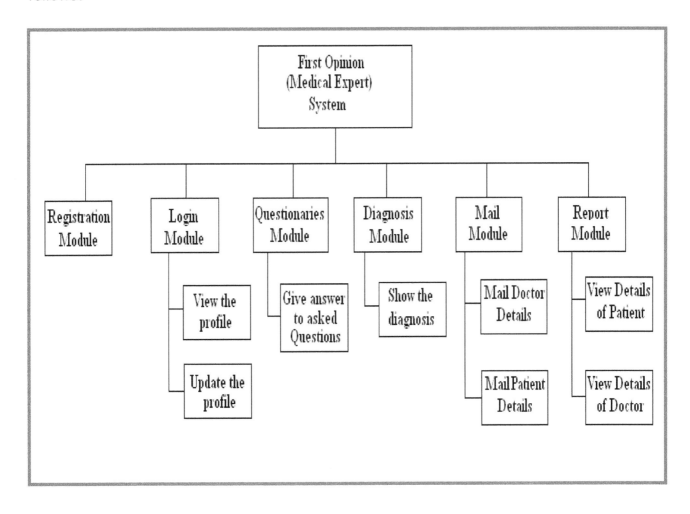

Case II: Draw FDD for Learning License Test System

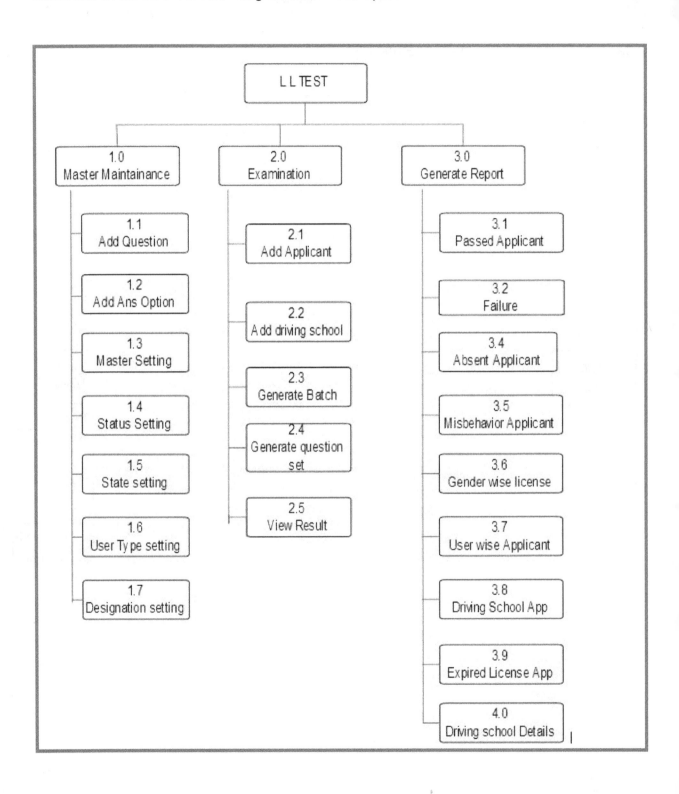

Case III: Draw FDD for Baby care Management System

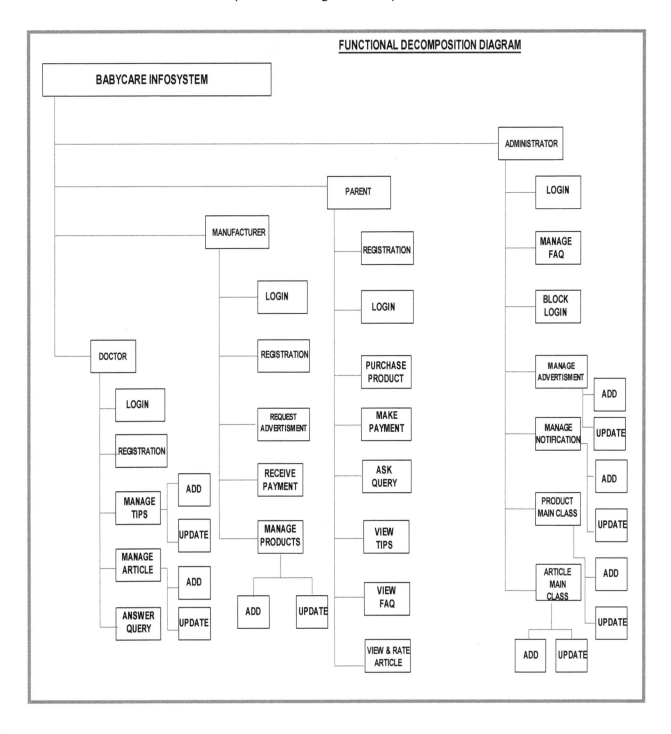

Case IV: Draw FDD for Logistic Monitoring System

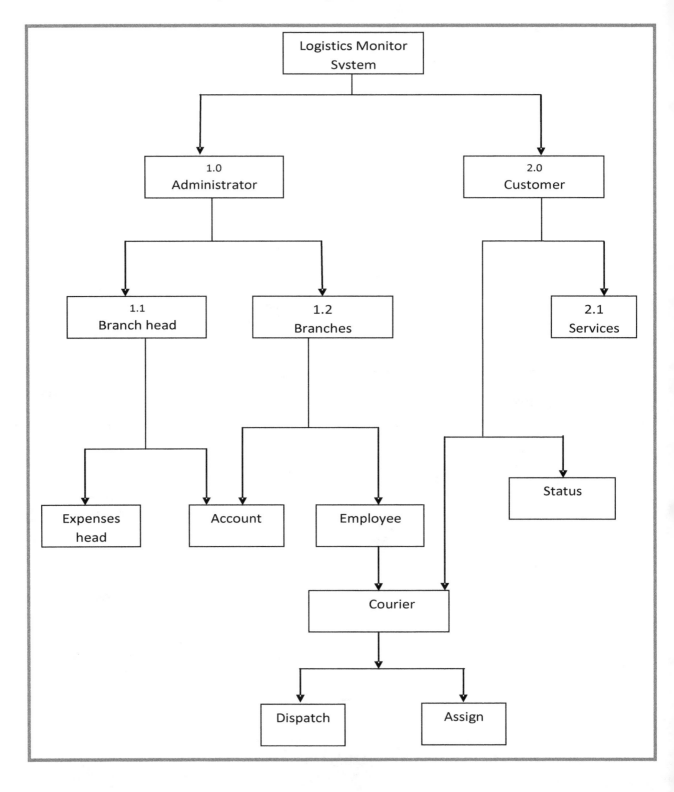

Case V: Draw FDD for Institute Marketing Management System

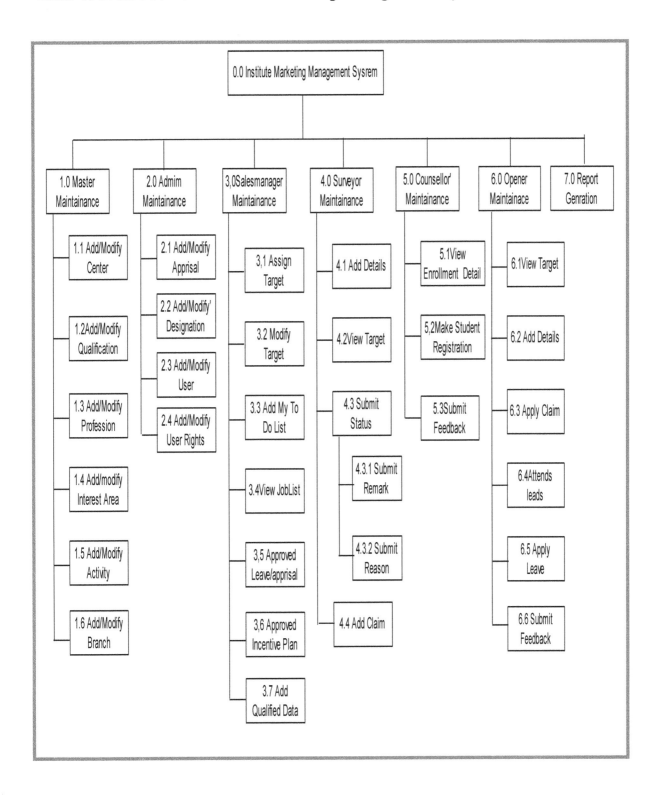

Case VI: Draw FDD for Merit Track System (Online Exam System)

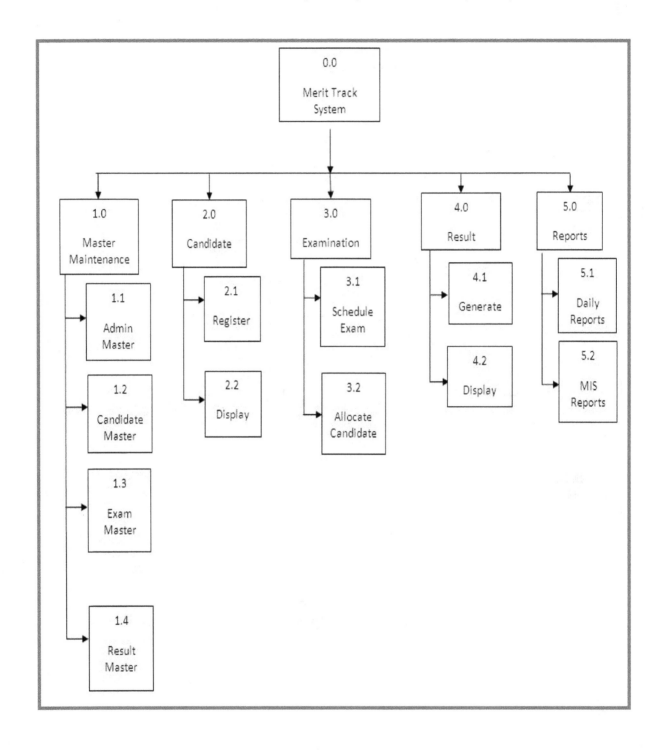

Case VII: Draw FDD for Electrical Management System for Contractor

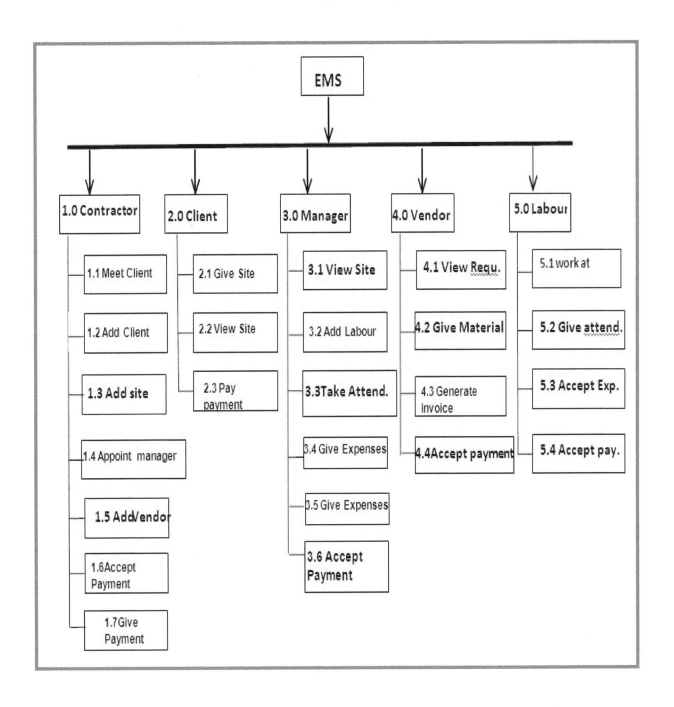

Case VIII: Draw FDD for E - FARMING

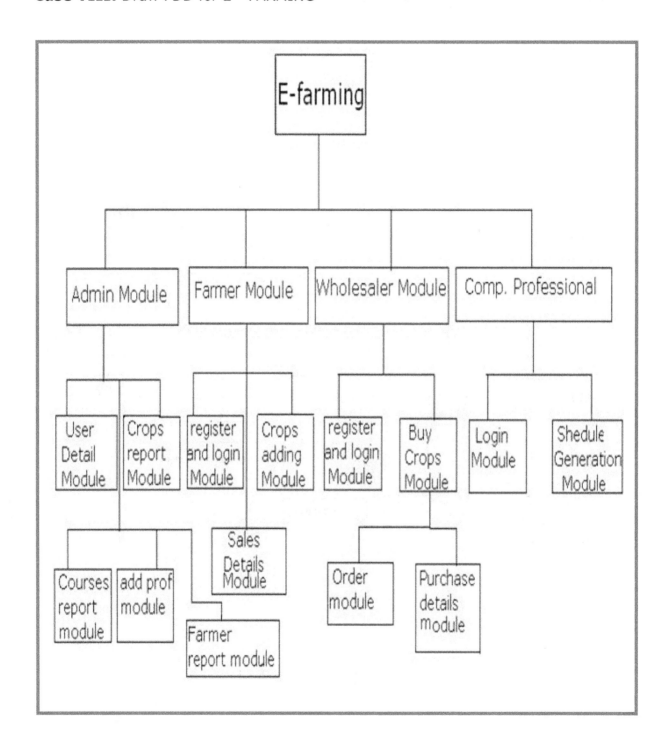

Case IX: Draw FDD for Housekeeping Management System

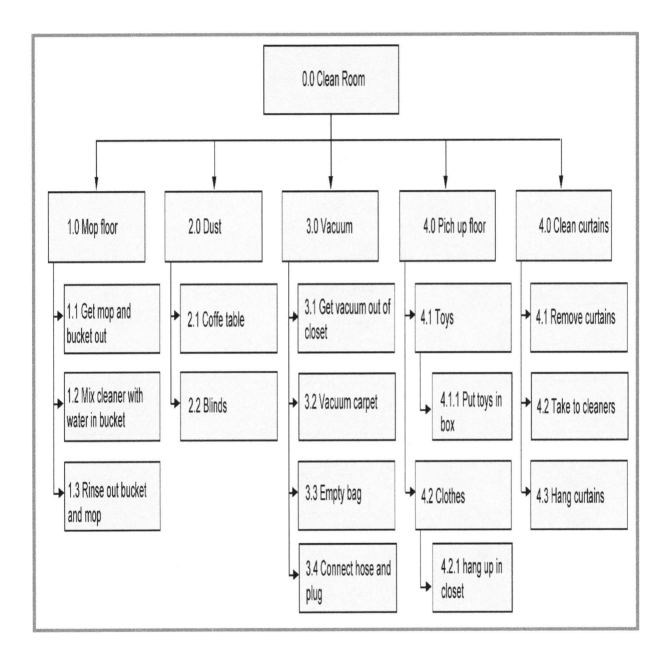

Case X: Draw FDD for Multimedia Kit Management System

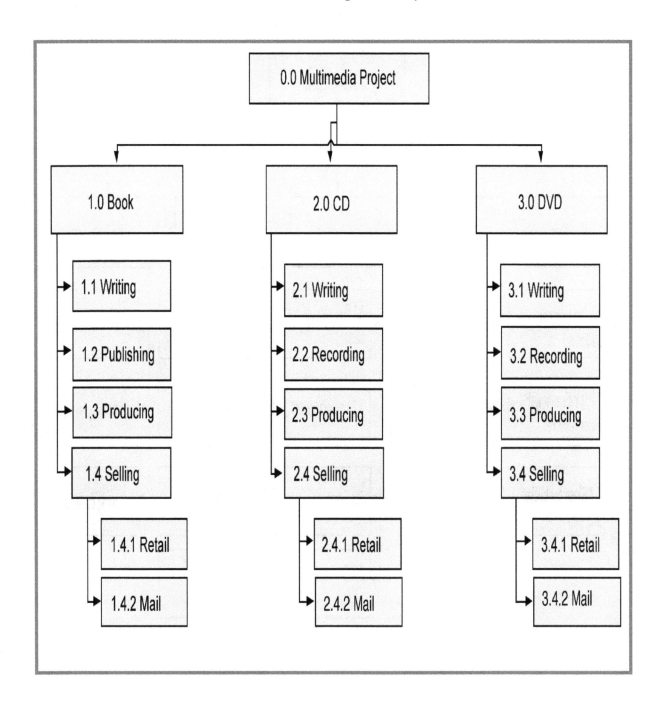

Topic 12. CASE STUDIES BASED ON DFD WITH LEVELS

❖ Tips to remember at the time of drawing D.F.D. :

➜ Firstly divide the whole system or application into number of subprocesses.

➜ Take every subprocesses sequentially in the DFD.

➜ At the time of drawing First levels of DFD, always remember that process should be connected or interrelated with each other with the help of Internal/External agent (Entity) and database. But don't connect subprocesses directly to each other by using arrows. But its allowed in Second level DFD.

➜ There should not be repetition of Internal/External agent(Entity) in drawing the various levels of DFD, Mostly in first level DFD.

➜ Internal/External agent (Enity) should be on left hand side of processes in first level DFD.

➜ Database should be on right hand side of processes in first level DFD.

➜ Draw various levels of DFD wherever necessary. Otherwise up to second level DFD is sufficient to describe the whole system.

➜ Give proper numbering to each and every subprocesses in specific format.

❖ Tricks to Solve Case (Draw DFD for given Case/System) :

➜ Read Case carefully and try to understand system in detail.

➜ Analyze & find out every subsystem or subprocess in the system.

➜ Use connectors in levels of DFD where your first level of DFD cannot fit in single page.

➜ Find out all Internal/External agents (Entity) and Tables(database) in complete system.

Case I: Draw Context level DFD for Medical Expert System

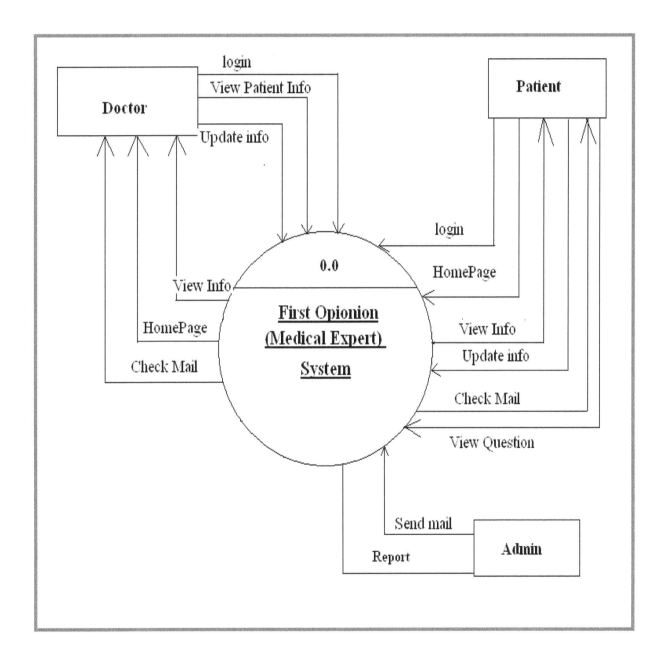

Case II: Draw Context level DFD, First and Second level of DFD for Learning License Test System

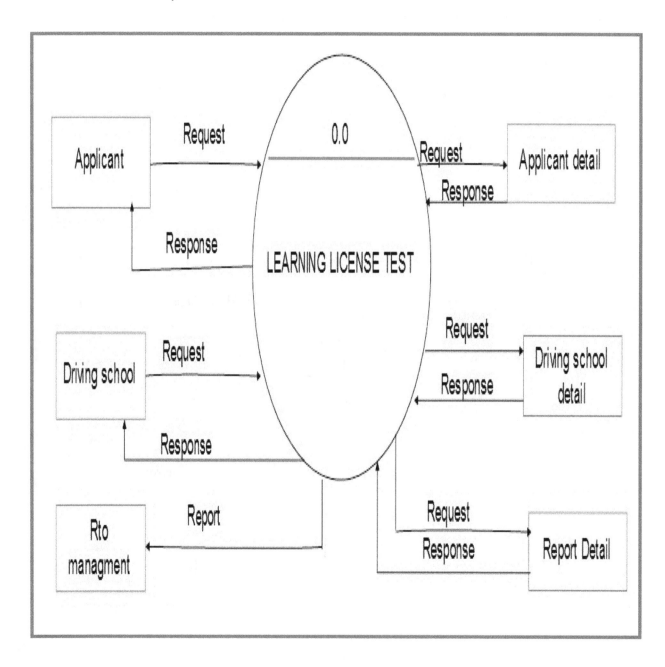

First Level of DFD (1st Level DFD) For Learning License Test System

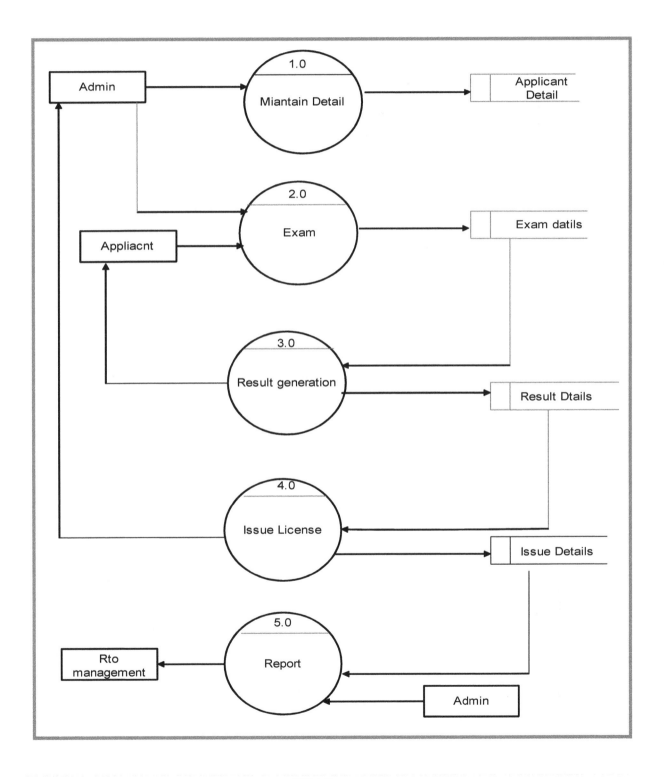

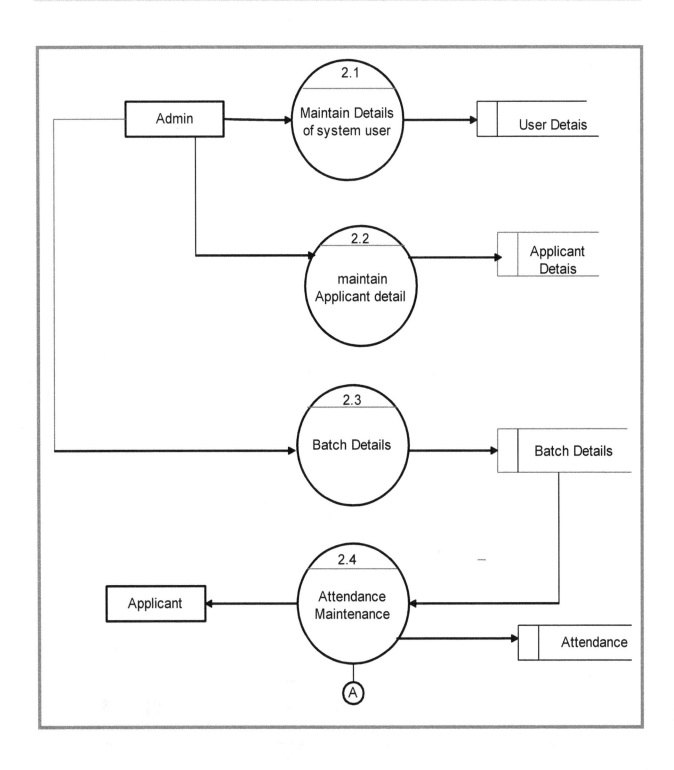

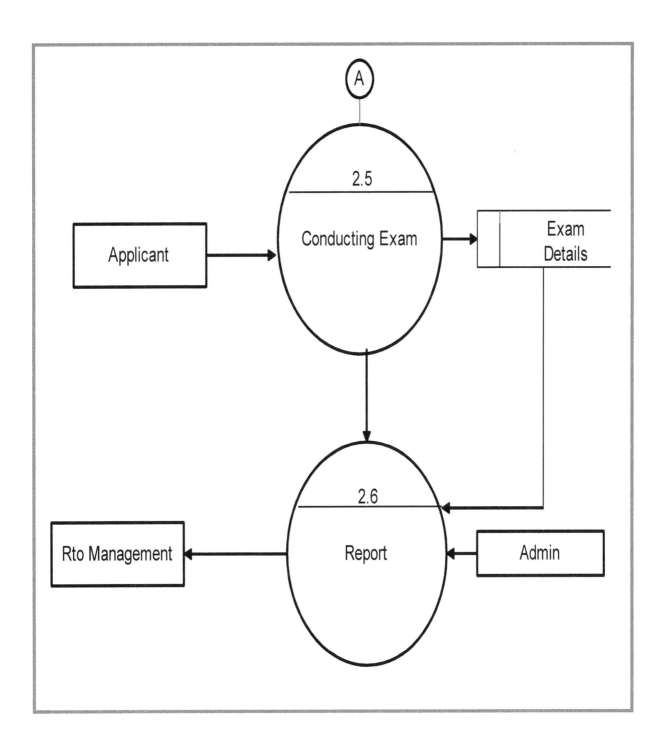

Case III: Draw Context level DFD for Digital Class System

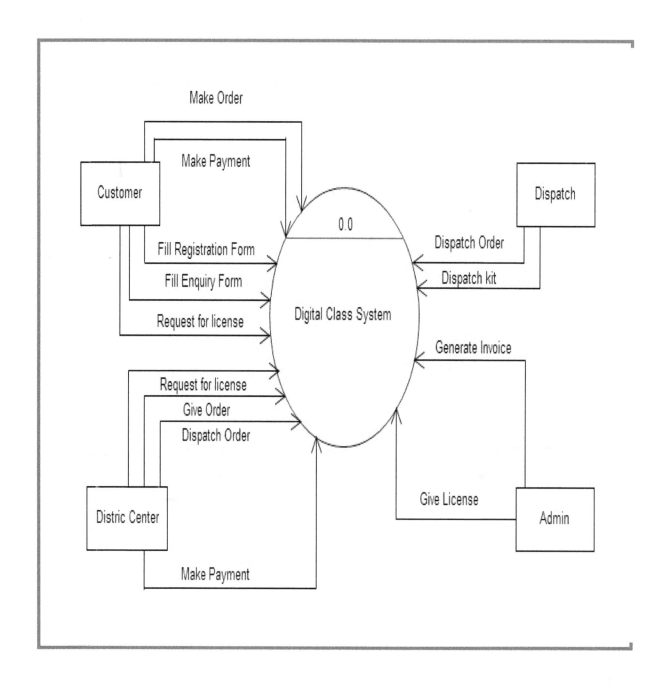

Case IV: Draw Context level DFD and First Level DFD for Logistic Monitoring

System

Context Level DFD For Logistic Monitoring System

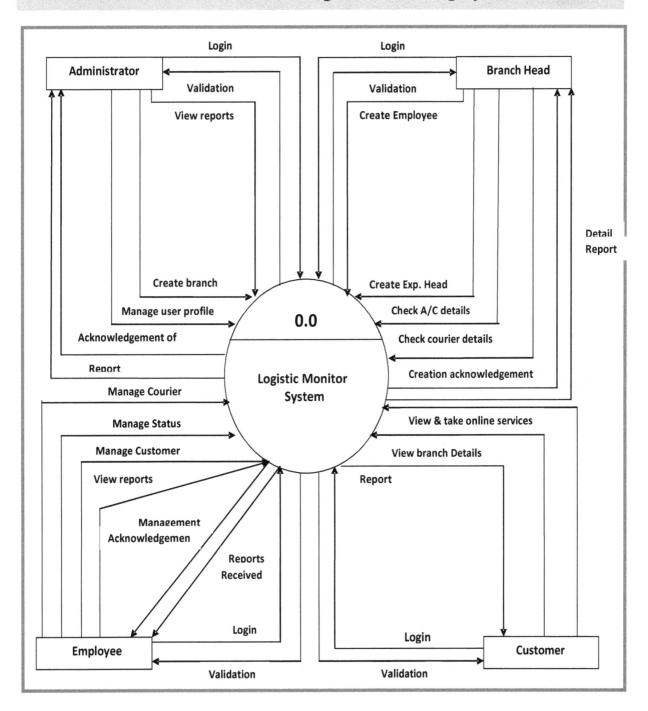

First Level DFD For Logistic Monitoring System

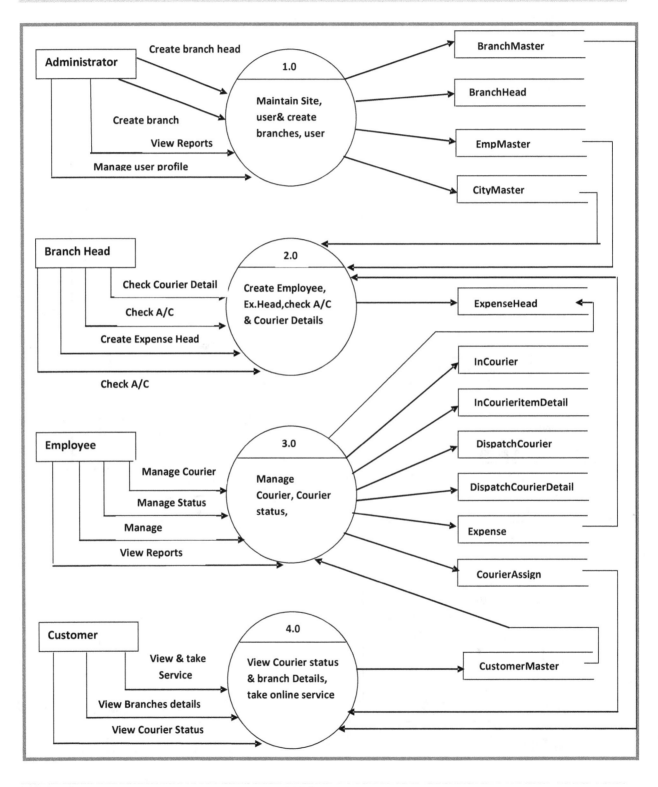

Case V: Draw Context level DFD for Baby Care Management System

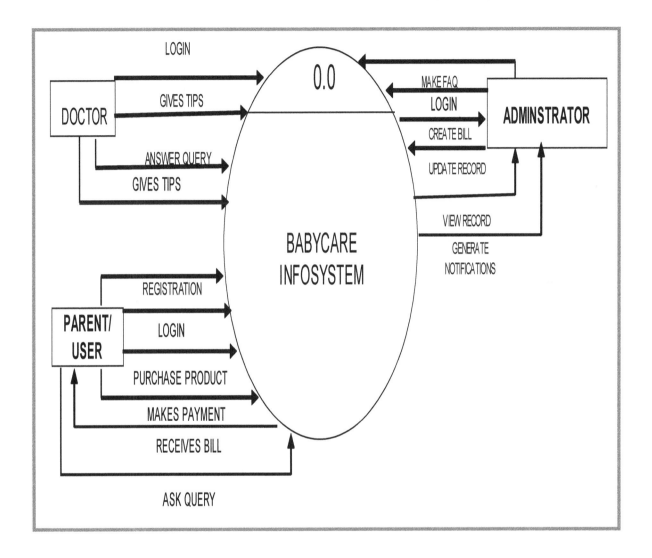

Case VI: Draw Context level & First Level DFD for Medicare Inventory System

Context Level DFD for Medicare Inventory System

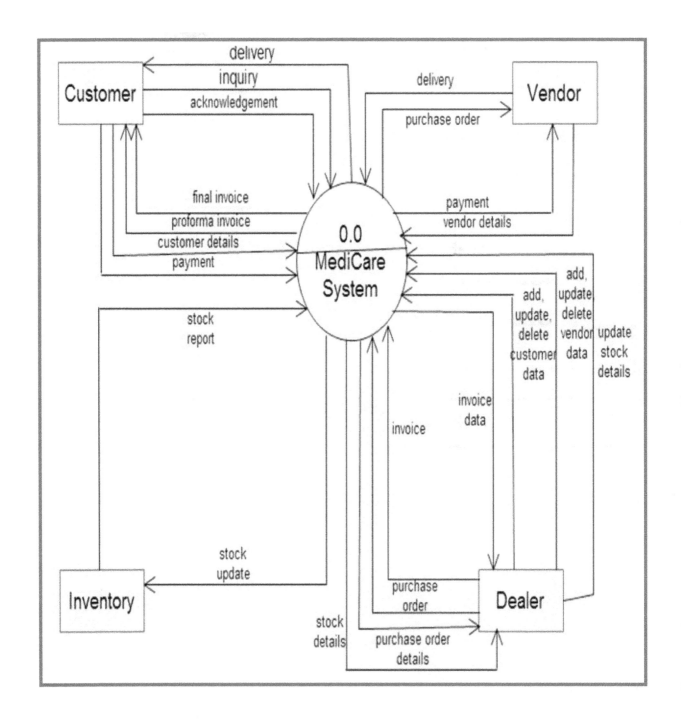

First Level DFD for Medicare Inventory System

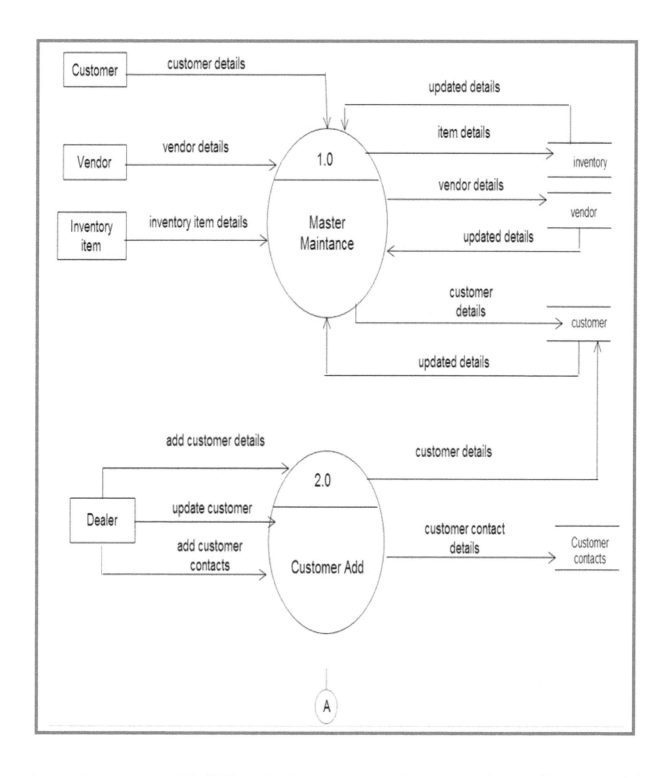

Continue…………………

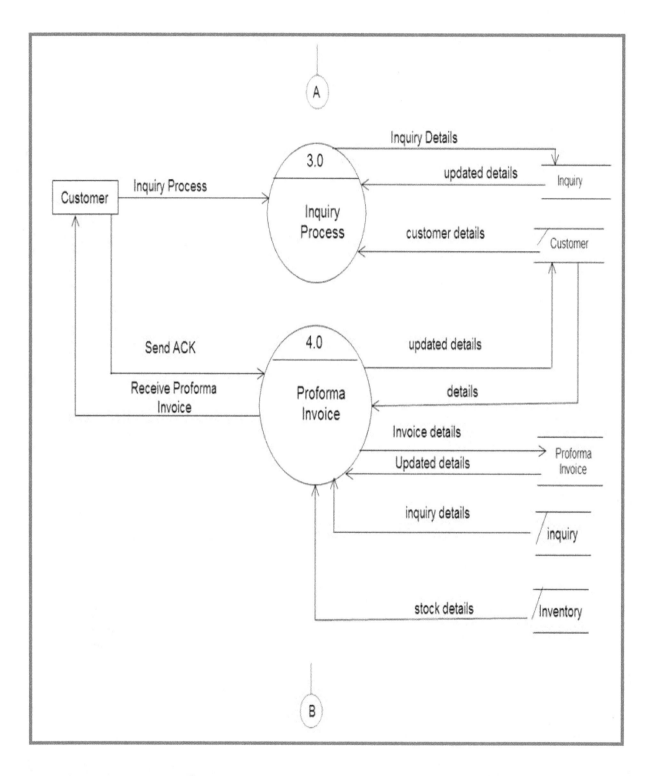

Continue…………………

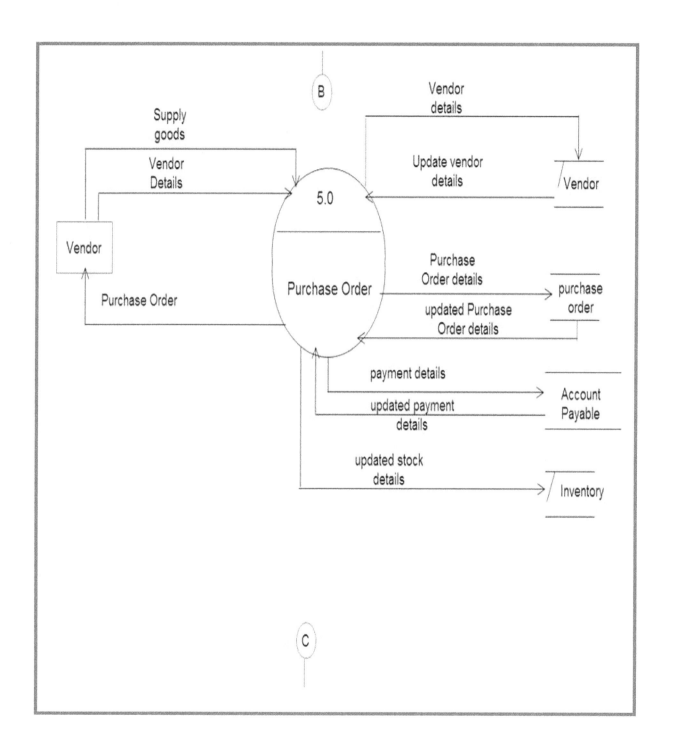

Continue…………………..

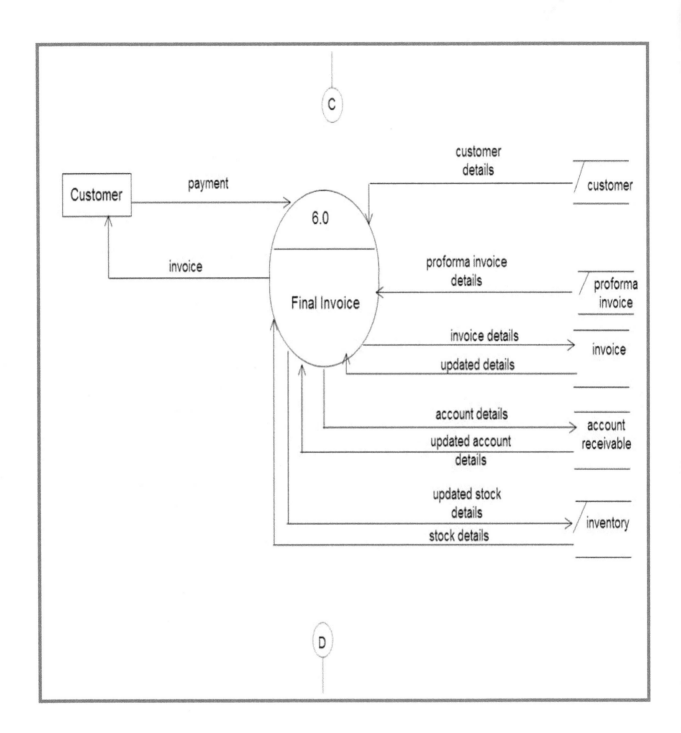

Continue…………………….

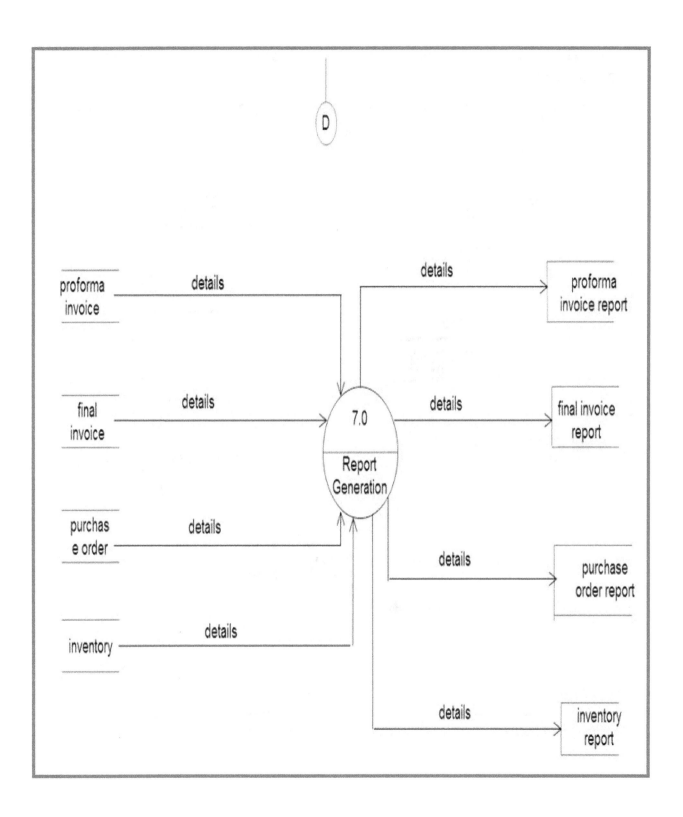

Case VII: Draw Context level & First Level DFD for Merit Track System (Online Exam System)

Context Level DFD for Merit Track System(Online Exam System)

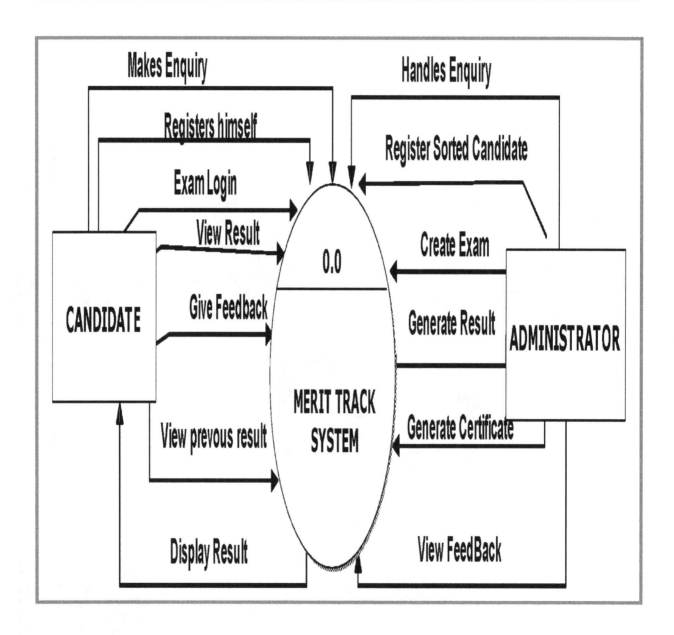

First Level DFD for Merit Track System(Online Exam System)

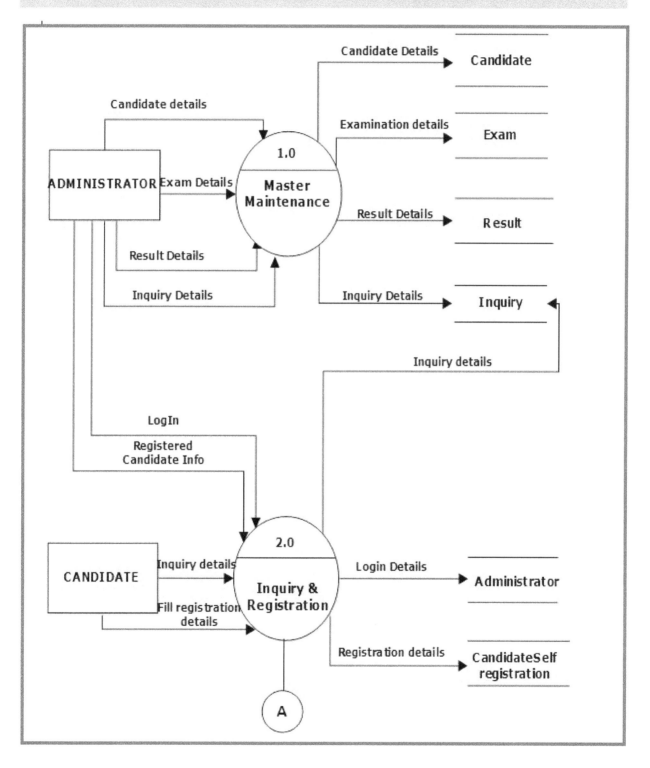

Continue…………………

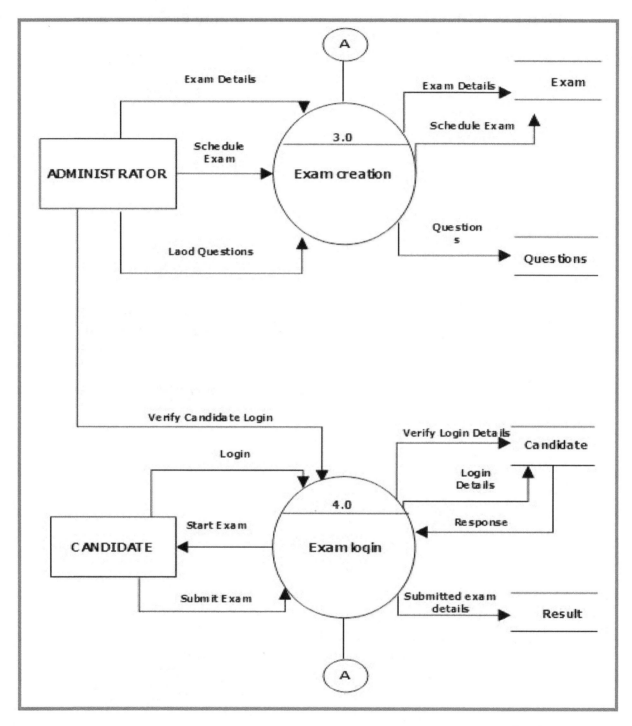

Continue……………

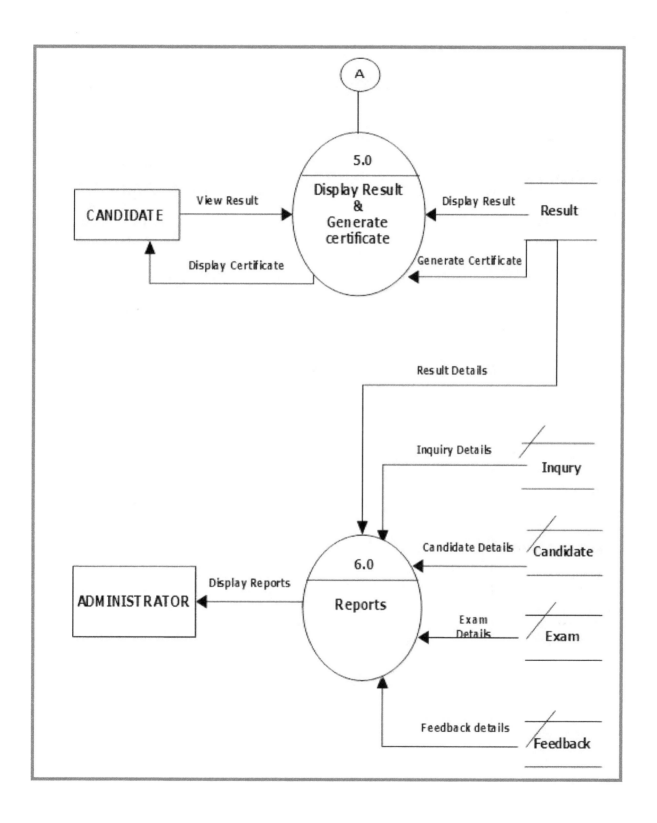

Case VIII: Draw Context level & First Level DFD for E- Farming

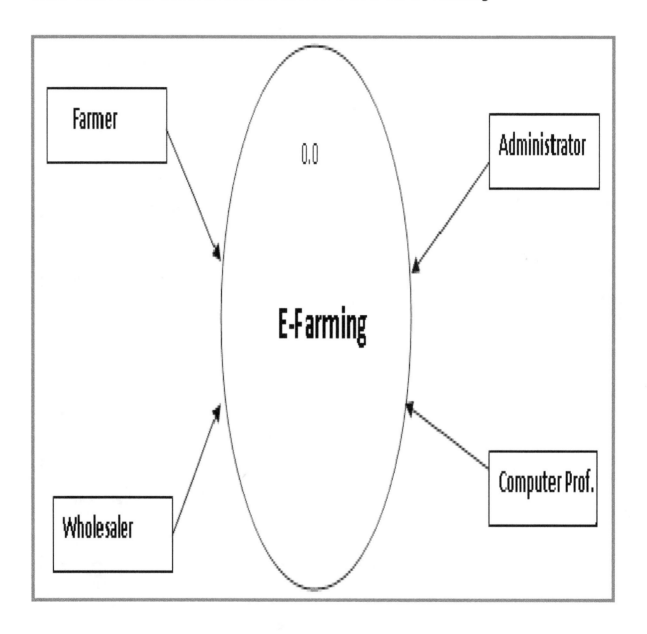

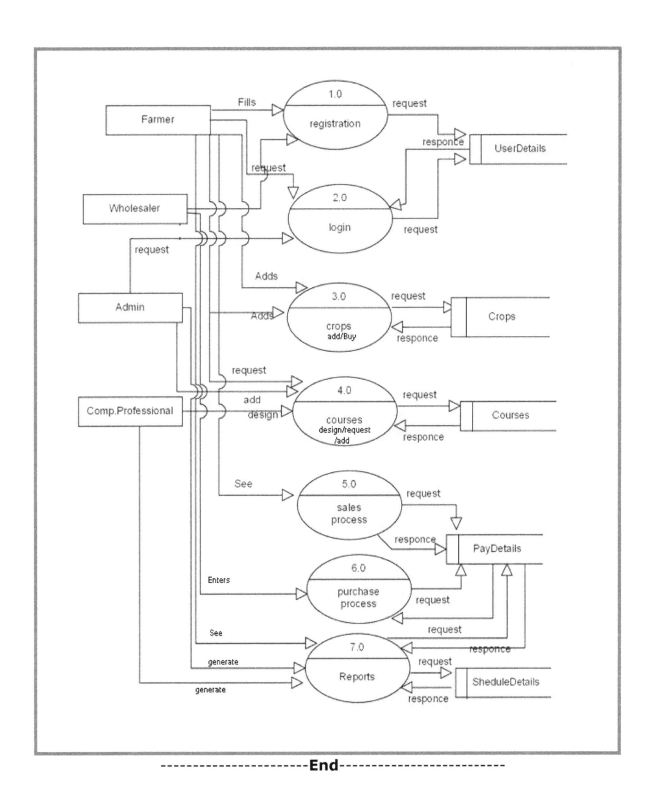

Note:

Topic 13. CASE STUDIES BASED ON S.R.S.

CASE I: It is decided to make College Library will available online to every user as well as students. In existing Library System there are number of limitations, but in new system launch with new functionality. So for this Online Library System prepare a well SRS having suitable structure.

Solution=>

As per we studied the SRS concept and structure of SRS in topic no. 9 we solve this case by following SRS format/structure with different sections as bellow:

1] Introduction:

Borrowing, returning and viewing the available books at the college library is currently done manually where the student has go to the library to do the book transactions. Student checks the list of available books and borrow it if it is not borrowed by any other else it is wastage of time for the student to come to the library. Then the librarian checks the student Id, allows him to check out the book and then updates the member and the books database. This takes at least one to two hours for the member to go to and complete his/her book transaction from the library.

1.1 Overview:

The proposed system would be Online Library Management System which would be used by member (student or faculty to check the availability and borrow the books and by the librarian to update the corresponding databases).

1.2   Purpose:

The purpose of SRS document is to describe the external behavior of the online library system – operations, interfaces, performance, quality assurance requirement and the design constraints. The SRS include the complete software requirements for the proposed system. The purpose of this SRS is to analyze the needs and features of this proposed online library system on high level.

1.3   Scope:

The online library system provides the members and employees of the library with all the books information, online blocking of books and many other facilities. The online library system will have the following features:

1. The system will be running 24 x 7.
2. Users can sign up and login to the system.
3. Members can check their accounts and change their password whenever needed.
4. The system allows the member to block the books 24 x 7 hours a day and all through the semester.
5. Library staff can check which members have blocked the books and whether they can borrow any more books or not.
6. Librarian can create and maintain the books catalog - add/delete books.
7. The system updates the billing system whenever a member borrows or returns a book.
8. We also have an order department which manages to add or remove a book from the library.

1.4 Definitions, Acronyms and Abbreviations:

- PIN :- Personal Identification Number.
- LAN :- Local Area Network.
- CLG :- college
- ASP :- Active Server pages.
- WWW :- World Wide Web.

1.5 References:

The SRS document uses the following Web and documents as references:

1. Various Online Portal for Financial Application.
2. Security present in existing Library System.
3. The billing system to provide the interface between the proposed system and the billing system currently in use by college to update the member account due whenever they borrow and return books.

2] Overall Description:

2.1 Product perspective:

The online library system is a software package that is useful to improve the efficiency of Libraries, Librarians and Users. The complete overview of the system is described in SRS as bellow. The proposed product has interaction with various kinds of users – Librarian, Students and Faculties of college.

The application/System has to interact with other systems also like: Internet, Billing System and the college information security system.

2.2 Product functions:

The product functions of the system describe the different types of services provided by the system based on the type of the users.

1. The member is provided with the updated information about the book catalog.
2. The members can borrow the books they want, if all the other required rules hold correct.
3. The members can check his/her account information and change it any time in the given valid duration.
4. The members are provided with the books catalog to choose the books which they need.
5. The librarian can get information about the members who have borrowed or returned the books.
6. The librarian can add/delete the books available in the book catalog.
7. The due to be paid by the member is calculated if in case he/she is late in submitting the books or fees.
8. The system uses the college information security requirements to provide the login facility to the users.

2.3 User Characteristics:

The users of the system are members and librarians of the college and administrative who maintain the system. The members and the librarian are assumed to have basic knowledge of the computers and Internet browsing. The administrators of the system have more knowledge about the internals of the system because he/she is responsible to rectify the system in cases of small problems that may arises due to disk crashes, power failures or any other disturbances.

2.4 General Constraints:

1. Information of all the users (Members & Librarians) must be stored in a database and that must be accessible by the proposed system.
2. College information security system must be compatible with the internet applications.
3. The online Library System should be running all 24 x 7 hours a day.
4. The users must be able to access the online library system from any computer that has internet connection.
5. The billing system is connected to the online library system and the database used by the billing system must be compatible the internet applications.
6. The users must be provided with correct username and password to login to the online library system.

2.5 Assumptions and Dependencies:
1. Users have basic knowledge of computers.
2. College computer should have internet connection and internet server capabilities.
3. User knew English language as the user interfaces is in English.
4. The proposed application software can access the college student database.

3] Specific Requirements:

3.1   External Interface Requirements:

3.1.1 User Interfaces:

Web Browsers: Microsoft Internet Explorer or Mozilla. The user Interface of the system shall be designed as shown in the user-Interface prototypes.

User-Interface Layout (Screen)

Note: - here you have to show or draw few user interfaces or screen by using pencil, scale etc. Screens like Login Screen, Home page etc.

Login Screen

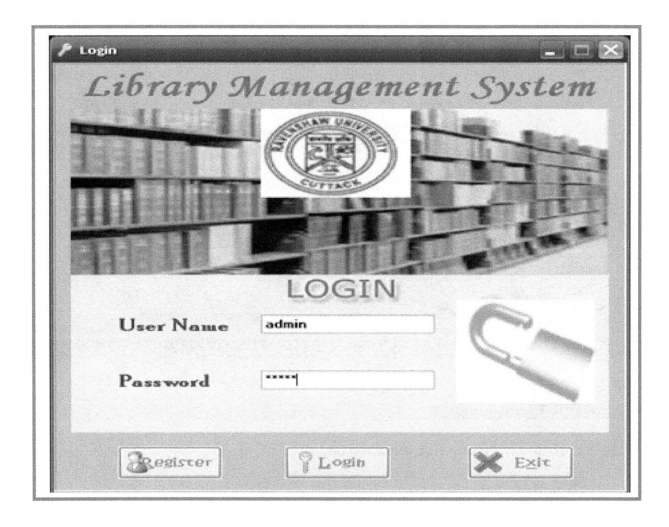

Home Page for Online Library Management System

RaDiX Library Management System 1.0

File About

Add Book | Add User | Search Book | Search User | Reports

Title

Author

Category   SN ▼   Book ID   10.4

Publisher

ISBN

Price

Other Details

Remove Book | Save Changes | Add Book | Cancel

User Category

Book Category

Database

Fines

Member Registration Screen

MEMBERSHIP

IdNo [   ]   Name [   ]

Address [   ]   Date Of Issue [   ]

Date Of Expiry [   ]   Status of Ms [   ]

Type of Ms [   ]   Amount [   ]

www.final-yearprojects.co.cc

[ADD]

Catalog Search page

3.1.2 Hardware Interfaces:

LAN will be used for collecting data from the users and also for updating the library catalogue.

3.1.3 Software Interfaces:

A firewall will be used with the server to prevent unauthorized access to the system.

3.1.4 Communication Interfaces:

The online library system will be connected to the WWW.

3.2 Functional Requirements:

The online library management system should fulfill all requirements of organization or users. The complete system is made up of different subsystem which will perform defined functionality. The functionality Requirements section consists of following validity checks:

1. The input screen where the all requirements are given.
2. The output screen which will give expected result required by the user.
3. The units of measure are checked at the time of giving input information by the user.
4. How the information gets processed is explained in the online library system.
5. Appropriate error messages are provided if any wrong input is given in the online library management system.
6. This functionality checks are available in each subparts or subsystem of whole online library system of college (i.e. modes of functionality requirements).

3.3 Performance Requirements:

The performance requirements for online library system can be measured in following way:

1. Login Capabilities: The system shall provide the users with login capabilities.
2. Mobile Devices: The Online Library System will also be supported on mobile devices such as cell phones.
3. Alerts: The system will alert the librarian or the Administrator in case of any problems.

4] Design Constraints:

1. Programming Language: The languages that will be used for coding the Online Library System are ASP.Net, HTML, JavaScript and VbScripts. To run the ASP pages the browsers should be properly configured.
2. Development Tool: We will make use of online references for developing the application in ASP, HTML, using the two scripting languages - JavaScript and VbScript.

5] Software System Attributes:

1. **Reliability:** The system has to be very much reliable to avoid the damages to data and prevent from entering incorrect or incomplete data.
2. **Availability:** The system is available to user all 24 x 7 hrs and 365 days a year.
3. **Security:** The system shall support the college information security requirements and use the same standard as the college information security requirements.
4. **Maintainability:** The maintenance of the system shall be done as per the maintenance contract.

5. **Portability:** The users will be able to access the online library system from any computer that has internet connection.

6. **Performance:**
   - Response Time: The information page should be able to be downloaded within second using a 56K Modem. The information is refreshed every two minutes. The response time for a mobile device must be less than a minute.
   - Throughput: The number of transactions is dependent on the number of the users.
   - Capacity: The system is capable of handling 200 users at a time.

6] Other Requirements:

1. **Licensing Requirements (EULA):**

   The usage is restricted to only College Library who is purchasing the Online Library System from software vendor and signs the maintenance contract.

2. **Applicable Standards:**

   The ISO/IEC guidelines for the documentation of computer based application systems will be followed.

7] Supporting Information:

The supporting information section includes as acceptance criteria. And the acceptance criteria are as follow.

Before accepting the system, the developer must demonstrate that the system works on the number of stock data, product, and quantity specification. The developer will have to show through test cases that all conditions are satisfied.

Also the developer must train to the user who will use online library system.

Note: This is compete SRS for Online Library System.

CASE II: Admission process of college consists of different processes. And if all this process works manually then student as well as college faces number of problems in complete admission system. The situation occurs like, in manual system minimum of 20 minutes is required for the clerk to verify the form, prepare fee receipt and collect cash/draft from that student. Due to that other student in the queue has to wait for their number, because of that some student may misbehave or complain. To solve all this problem college management has decided to make Computerized Admission System or Process (CAP). So prepare a well structured SRS for such system.

Solution=>

As per we studied the SRS concept and structure of SRS in topic no. 9 we solve this case by following SRS format/structure with different sections as bellow:

1] Introduction:

Computerized Admission System is automated system that will be minimize the time required for the admission procedure and hence the wait time of the student and also minimize the problem during admission procedure.

1.6 Overview:

The proposed system would be prepare a merit list, fee structure and other information in less time saving system the time of the student and clerk in preparing the merit list. It will give timely information about admission status to the student and answer queries by the student or guardian.

1.7   Purpose:

The purpose of this SRS is to define the requirements for the computerized admission procedure of a college. In detail, this document will provide a general description of our project including product perspective, overview of requirements, general constraints and user view of product use. In addition, it will also provide specific requirements and functionality needed for this project such as interface.

1.8   Scope:

CAP is an automated system that will assist the college administration to admit students to various courses offered by the college with least paper work required and least time consumed for the student and the clerk during the admission process. The online library system will have the following features:

9. The system will save time and reduce conflicts.
10. Users can sign up and login to the system.
11. Administrators can check their accounts and change their password whenever needed.
12. The system updates the fees detail whenever a student will take admission.
13. The system will update student information whenever student confirm or cancel the admission.

1.9   Definitions, Acronyms and Abbreviations:
- ADM :- Admission.
- ACK :- Acknowledgement.
- Can Fee :- Cancelation Fee.
- I-Card :- Identity Card.
- Gym :- Gymnasium.
- CAP :- Computerized Admission Process.

1.10 References:

The SRS document uses the following Web and documents as references:

4. Various Online Portal for Online Admission System.
5. Security present in existing Admission System.
6. The Fee Collection system to provide the interface between the proposed system and the fees collection system currently in use by college to update the student account due whenever they take or cancel admission.

2] Overall Description:

2.1 Product perspective:

The CAP system is a software package that is useful to improve the efficiency of College Management. The complete overview of the system is as described in the SRS. The proposed product has interaction with various kinds of users – Student, College office Staff and Management of college.

The application/System has to interact with other systems also like: Internet, Fees Collection System and the college information security system.

2.2 Product functions:

The product functions of the system describe the different types of services provided by the system based on the type of the users.

9. The student is provided with the updated information about the courses and fee structure.
10. The administrator can check student information and change it any time in the given valid duration.

11. The librarian can get information about the members who have borrowed or returned the books.
12. The college clerk can add/delete the student details course wise.
13. The due to be paid by the student is calculated if in case he/she is late in submitting the fees in installment.
14. The system uses the college information security requirements to provide the login facility to the administrator.

2.3 User Characteristics:

The users of the system are clerk and of the college and administrative who maintain the system. The clerk and the administrator are assumed to have basic knowledge of the computers and Internet browsing. The administrators of the system have more knowledge about the internals of the system because he/she is responsible to rectify the system in cases of small problems that may arises due to disk crashes, power failures or any other disturbances.

2.4 General Constraints:

7. Information of all the users (students & administrators) must be stored in a database and that must be accessible by the proposed system.
8. The proposed system in not a web application but will work in intranet.
9. The users must be able to access the CAP system from any computer that has in LAN connection.
10. The fees collection system is connected to the computerized admission system and the database used by the fees collection system must be compatible.

11.The Administrators must be provided with correct username and password to login to the CAP system.

2.5 Assumptions and Dependencies:

5. Users have basic knowledge of computers.
6. College computers should have LAN connection and Client-Server capabilities.
7. User knew English language as the user interfaces is in English.
8. The proposed application software can access the college student database.

3] Specific Requirements:

3.1 External Interface Requirements:

3.1.1 User Interfaces:

Operating System: Microsoft operating system i.e. Windows 98 and above. The user Interface of the system shall be designed as shown in the user- Interface prototypes.

Note: - here you have to show or draw few user interfaces or screen by using pencil, scale etc. Screens like Login Screen, student information etc.

Login Screen

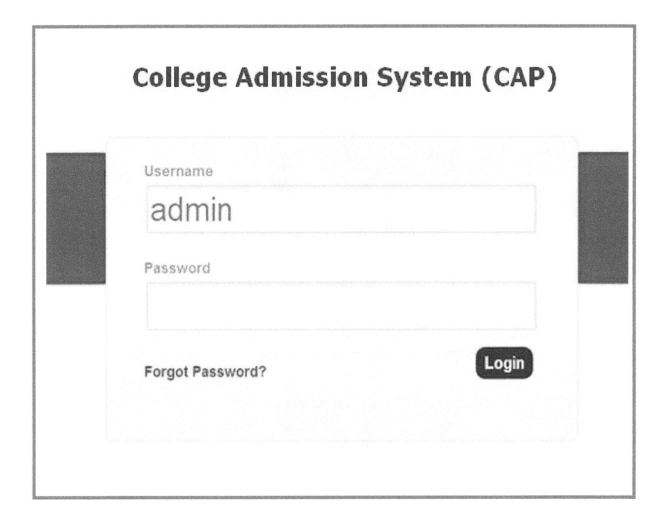

College Admission System (CAP) Main GUI

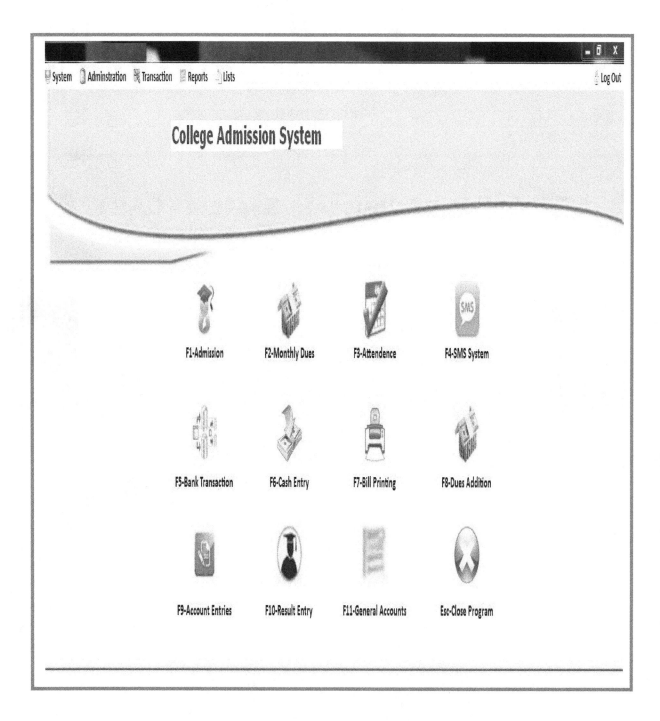

New Student Admission Entry Screen

New Admission

Adm. No : **3004922** * Course Code : 0   Adm. Date : 25-12-2012   *

dd-mm-yyyy

Student's Name : _____   * Date Of Birth : _ _ _ _ _

Father's Name : _____   *   Gender : Male ▾

Address : _____   Phone 1 : 0

*

Phone 2 : 0

Select Picture

Reset

Class : PLAY GROUP ▾   Section : A ▾

Adm. Fee : 0	Lab Fee : 0	Hostel Fee : 0	Syllabus : 0
Security : 0	Comp Fee : 0	Lunch Fee : 0	Photostate : 0
Monthly Fee : 0	Van Charges : 0	Exam Fee : 0	Other Charges : 0

Concession : 0

LAST ADMISSION

F12   F5   Esc

💾 Save   ✓ Clear   ✗ Close

Student Fee Collection Interface Screen

Student Fee Collection Analysis

| By Name | By Father | By Adm. No | By D.O.B | By Class | By Section | By Family | By Phone |

Name : [   ]   Students : [0]

Student's Name	Adm No.	Father's Name	Address

Adm. No : [0]   Family Code : [0]   Adm. Date : [- -]

Student's Name : [   ]   Date Of Birth : [- -]

Father's Name : [   ]   Gender : [   ]

Address : [   ]   Phone 1 : [0]

Phone 2 : [0]

Class : [   ]

Adm. Fee :	0	Lab Fee :	0	Photostate :	0	Van Charges :	0
Monthly Fee :	0	Exam Fee :	0	Lunch Fee :	0	Security :	0
Comp Fee :	0	Books :	0	Hostel Fee :	0	Concession :	0

Esc
✕ Close

3.1.2 Hardware Interfaces:

LAN will be used for collecting data from the users and also for updating the student information.

3.1.3 Software Interfaces:

A firewall will be used with the server to prevent unauthorized access to the system.

3.1.4 Communication Interfaces:

The Computerized Admission system will be connected in the Intranet architecture.

3.2 Functional Requirements:

The CAP system should fulfill all requirements of organization or users. The complete system is made up of different subsystem which will perform defined functionality. The functionality Requirements section consists of following validity checks:

7. The input screen where the all requirements are given.
8. The output screen which will give expected result required by the user.
9. The CAP system will reduce the paper work and save the time of student.
10. How the information gets processed is explained in the CAP system.
11. Appropriate error messages are provided if any wrong input is given in the Computerized Admission system.
12. This functionality checks are available in each subparts or subsystem of whole CAP system of college (i.e. modes of functionality requirements).
13. CAP system will simplify the admission procedure.

3.3   Performance Requirements:

The performance requirements for CAP system can be measured in following way:

4. Login Capabilities: The system shall provide the users with login capabilities.
5. Fast execution: The CAP System will process student information rapidly required for admission.
6. Alerts: The system will alert the librarian or the Administrator in case of any problems.

4] Design Constraints:

3. Programming Language: The languages that will be used for coding the CAP System are VB.Net, ASP.Net.
4. Database: The CAP System maintain the huge students information so it is better to use SQL or Oracle as backend as security point view.

5] Software System Attributes:

7. **Reliability:** The system has to be very much reliable to avoid the damages to data and prevent from entering incorrect or incomplete data.
8. **Availability:** The system is available to user whenever login into the system.
9. **Security:** The system shall support the college information security requirements and use the same standard as the college information security requirements.
10. **Maintainability:** The maintenance of the system shall be done as per the maintenance contract.
11. **Portability:** The users will be able to access the CAP system from any computer that has in LAN.

6] Other Requirements:

3. Licensing Requirements (EULA):

The usage is restricted to only College Administration who is purchasing the CAP System from software vendor and signs the maintenance contract.

4. Applicable Standards:

The ISO/IEC guidelines for the documentation of computer based application systems will be followed.

7] Supporting Information:

The supporting information section includes as acceptance criteria. And the acceptance criteria are as follow.

Before accepting the system, the developer must demonstrate that the system works on the number of stock data, product, and quantity specification. The developer will have to show through test cases that all conditions are satisfied.

Also the developer must train to the user who will use Computerized Admission system.

Note: This is compete SRS for Computerized Admission System.

----------------------End------------------------

Topic 14. CASE STUDY QUESTION BANK.

Q: For the following Systems draw the ERD, FDD, DFD and levels of DFD, Decision Tree & Create Database Design, Data Dictionary:

Q: Prepare the Software Requirement Specification for following Systems:

1 Attendance Management System

2 online recruitment system(ORS)

3 Network Traffic Analysis

4 courier management service

5 controlling a pc using a mobile phone

6 Super Market Management System (SMMS)

7 computer institute management system

8 Online Consultancy

9 Computerizing the Student Registration System

10 E-bazaar

11 virtual classroom

12 Student management system

13 intranet mail server

14 University Admission System

15 Library Management system

16 Vehicle Access Control

17 SECURITY SYSTEM USING IP CAMERA

18 human resource administration System

19 peer 2 peer multimedia transmission

20 remote server room control through web

21 face recognition

22 online shopping

23 Rendering 3D images on 2D display

24 System for online customer service

25 online activity monitor

26 mail++ A Webmail Service (JSP)

27 distance learning system

28 TCP/IP messenger chat, voip, video, file copy...

29 Employee Management System

30 inventory management system/Purchase order system

31 online exams

32 2 D GRAPHIS EDITOR

33 airline reservation System

34 hospital management System

35 Electronic Document Manager

36 I-Voting

37 Hostel management system

38 core banking System

39 online banking

40 web editor in java

41 web speed enhancer

42 e-post office system

43 school management system

44 school fees payment system

45 hotel reservation System

46 ticket reservation

47 System for Trading-Tax
48 Graphical editor

49 canteen management System

50 Bus reservation system

51 E-mail System

52 Online Credit card payment systems

53 management of internet cafe

54 Online Share Trading System

55 online objective test

56 Supply Chain Management System

57 ERP (Enterprise resource planning) System for Domain

58 Emergency Health care System

59 online car sales and purchasing

60 online telephone billing system(ASP.Net, C#)

61 System gas booking

62 MYJOBS.COM

63 Image processing

64 Bank loan system in .NET

65 Pharmaceutical projects

Online Application / System (WEB SITES)

1 Web site for courier Services

2 Mobile Product Web Portal

3 Web Site For online Shopping

4 Jobs Web Portal

5 Web site for buying or selling Vehicle

6 Web Site for Computer Shoppe

7 Online Examination Web site

8 Web Site for Airline Services

9 Web Portal for Medicare/Hospital

10 Web Site for Banking Domain

11 Web portal for Railway reservation system

12 Web site for Advertisement of Products(Ele,Cosm. Etc)

13 Web site for trading

14 Web site for Institutes

15 Web site Organization(eg. Construction, Press)

16 Web site for E-News Paper

17 Web Portal for GIS (Graphical Information System)

18 Matrimonial Web Site

19 Astrological Web Site

20 Web Site Government (E-Governance)

21 Online Search Engine (eg. GOOGLE,YAHOO etc)

22 Online Library Web Portal

23 Online E-Learning web site

24 Online Programming Tutorials

25 Web site for Gaming Zone

26 Web Site for Online Multimedia Library(eg. CD/DVD etc)

27 Web site for Online Admission

28 Web site for Tourism Services

29 Computer Shoppe Web Portal

30 Web Portal for E-Agriculture

-----------------------**End**-------------------------

Note:

www.ingramcontent.com/pod-product-compliance
Lightning Source LLC
Chambersburg PA
CBHW080554060326
40689CB00021B/4852